WITHDRAWN

THE AUGUST WILSON CENTURY CYCLE

RADIO GOLF

1997

THE AUGUST WILSON CENTURY CYCLE

RADIO GOLF

1997

AUGUST WILSON

FOREWORD BY SUZAN-LORI PARKS

THEATRE COMMUNICATIONS GROUP
NEW YORK
2007

The August Wilson Century Cycle is published by Theatre Communications Group, Inc.,
520 Eighth Avenue, 24th Floor, New York, NY 10018-4156

The August Wilson Century Cycle is funded in part by the Ford Foundation, with additional support from The Paul G. Allen Family Foundation, The Heinz Endowments
and the New York State Council on the Arts.

TCG books are exclusively distributed to the book trade by Consortium Book Sales
and Distribution, 1045 Westgate Drive, St. Paul, MN 55114.

LIBRARY OF CONGRESS CATALOGING-IN-PUBLICATION DATA
Wilson, August.
Radio golf / by August Wilson ; foreword by Suzan-Lori Parks.—1st ed.
p. cm.—(August Wilson century cycle)
ISBN-13: 978-1-55936-306-8 (vol.)
ISBN-10: 1-55936-306-1 (vol.)
ISBN-13: 978-1-55936-307-5 (set)
ISBN-10: 1-55936-307-X (set)
1. African Americans—Drama. 2. Nineteen nineties—Drama. 3. Hill District
(Pittsburgh, Pa.)—Drama. 4. Real estate development—Drama. 5. African American
neighborhoods—Drama. I. Title.
PS3573.I45677R33   2007
812'.54—dc22   2007022085

Text design and composition by Lisa Govan
Slipcase and cover design by John Gall
Cover photograph by Peter Diana/*Pittsburgh Post-Gazette*
Slipcase photographs by Dana Lixenberg (author) and David Cooper

First Edition, September 2007

To Benjamin Mordecai,
who was there from the beginning—
good company, a friend, a brother

FOREWORD

by Suzan-Lori Parks

In the twenty-first century we can go forward together.
That was my idea behind the play.

—AUGUST WILSON

Dear Mr. August Wilson:

Congratulations on your play, your *Radio Golf*, your
10th in your "epic century cycle" as the academy might
claim it, and, as the corner might claim it: "We at
AW's number 10! Number 10 in his mad crazy all
that / big X / and who the hell he think he is, oh, you
know / AW the man who lay it down / AW give us
some places at The Table / AW made a 10-pack of
constellations with our names writ all over them / he
doing that apotheosis thing." You've brought us together
with an embrace of love—like a grandmother's hug:

> *I'm gonna love you*
> *All the way through.*

This 10th of your talented 10th
this 10 of your big 10
this X of your X
this spot marker
this dig-here-and-find-the-treasure play
this no-I-ain't-playing play
this I-have-a-dream play
this we-are-such-stuff-as-dreams-are-made-of play
this grapes-not-raisins-in-the-sun play
this 10-more-reasons-why-everybody-wanna-be-black-and-
    proud play
this song of songs
this road
this way
this gift
this *Radio Golf*.

Golf on the radio? Sounds crazy. Just like black folks on the golf course in great numbers sounded crazy a few years ago. Crazy for real.

When we spoke in August of 2005 for *American Theatre*, you said,

> One of the things with *Radio Golf* is that I realized
> I had to in some way deal with the black middle class,
> which for the most part is not in the other nine plays.
> My idea was that the black middle class seems to be
> divorcing themselves from that community, making
> their fortune on their own without recognizing or
> acknowledging their connection to the larger commu-
> nity. And I thought: We have gained a lot of sophisti-
> cation and expertise and resources, and we should be
> helping that community, which is completely devas-
> tated by drugs and crime and the social practices of

the past hundred years of the country. I thought: How
do I show that you can go back and that you can't—

Here are some things I love about *Radio Golf*:

TIGERS AND NIGGERS AND NEGROES AND KINGS

Roosevelt puts a picture of Tiger Woods on the wall; Harmond hangs up a poster of Dr. King. Mr. Woods and Dr. King are two bright lights leading us on. They stand up and stand out and fight the power. But are they "Negroes" or "niggers"? Depends where you're at, I guess. Sterling calls Roosevelt a Negro:

> STERLING: You know what you are? . . . You a Negro
> . . . I'm a nigger . . . It's Negroes like you who hold
> us back.

Sterling hits a home run with that line, drawing a brand-new color line, which goes deeper than skin. And with that line we can also imagine hearing Sterling's old prison pals calling him "Negro" and Roosevelt's new golf pals calling him (behind his back) "nigger." The play is filled with ways to be, paths to choose. The time has come to pick sides.

REDEVELOPMENT

Your characters Harmond and Mame and Roosevelt—they've made it. They *got*. They got cars and houses and businesses and jobs. They got and get welcomed to The Table. Roosevelt, the VP at the bank, plays golf with his wealthy white friends; Harmond's got a thriving real-estate development business; Mame's about to be offered a job by the governor.

In this play, even your less well-off characters got something (even your poorest were never totally without). Sterling's got carpentry skills that help him build solid steps away from his prison record; Elder Joseph (Old Joe) Barlow's got the house on Wylie. And while Harmond, Roosevelt and Mame are living on Easy Street, the living isn't always easy.

Harmond and Roosevelt have a plan to redevelop the historic Hill District. Will 1839 Wylie remain standing or will Harmond's redevelopment project tear it down? And as the play unfolds, "redevelopment" means more than fixing up some buildings—not just redeveloping the neighborhood, but redeveloping the people, too. We've developed. We've struggled and come through, and now we got some redeveloping to do. At the end of the play when Harmond grabs a paintbrush so that he can help restore the house at 1839 Wylie Avenue, we all know there's more than just a paint job that's needed. We need to restore ourselves to OurSelves—to see ourselves in the Other, to welcome the brother.

BREAD PUDDING

HARMOND: I have something for you.
OLD JOE: It ain't no bread pudding, is it? I was just thinking about some bread pudding. You like bread pudding?

This is a delicious moment. Harmond is about to hand Old Joe Barlow a big check, but Barlow's interest in a different kind of bread—bread pudding—sends the forward movement of the play and the onward and upward movement of the redevelopment project into a wild spin. Those "bread pudding" moments fight to be heard amidst the bustle and roar of Harmond's busy schedule and fight to be included within the dramaturgical demands of the "well-made play" just as 1839 Wylie fights to remain standing alongside the grand development plans. We're reminded that the people involved are larger and more complicated structures than those of buildings or plays. The bread pudding moment might not survive the dramaturg's test—they'd suggest you cut it, just like the renovation project suggests, "Tear down that house on Wylie." And yet you find a way to let both stand. To me that's radical dramaturgy. Mr. Wilson, you are wild in ways that people aren't even hip to. You've got a lot of *bread pudding* going on and it's thrilling. Within the lines of this play, you've made a place for the unconventional, the bit that does not traditionally fit, the outsider, the digression, the seemingly extraneous. Plays are supposed to be *structured* just as development projects are supposed to be *structured*, and Old Joe Barlow just rambles— seeming not to be saying anything. As you said when we spoke,

> The bread pudding is saying, "Wait a minute, there's a history here and it doesn't fit in with you guys' stuff." The bread pudding is not part of the traditional structure of the play, but it's part of the structure of this particular community backed up against change.

In performances to come—and there will be many—I invite people to see and revel in the *bread pudding*. I would encourage people to *rave* in the nonlinearity of your well-made plots, to *big-up* your quirky architecture, to *honor guard* the house at 1839 Wylie so that it will always remain standing. That house, and the ground on which it stands, will open doorways to others.

I'm picking up my paintbrush.

Miss You, Peace,
S-L P

Suzan-Lori Parks is a playwright, novelist and screenwriter who was awarded the 2002 Pulitzer Prize for Drama for Topdog/Underdog. *In August 2005, a few months before his death, she conducted an interview with August Wilson for* American Theatre *magazine. The interview was published in November 2005.*

RADIO GOLF

1997

Radio Golf premiered on April 22, 2005, at the Yale Repertory Theatre (James Bundy, Artistic Director; Victoria Nolan, Managing Director) in New Haven, Connecticut. It was directed by Timothy Douglas; the set design was by David Gallo, the costume design was by Susan Hilferty, the lighting design was by Donald Holder, the sound design was by Vincent Olivieri; the stage manager was Narda E. Alcorn and the dramaturg was Todd Kreidler. The cast was as follows:

HARMOND WILKS	Richard Brooks
MAME WILKS	Michele Shay
ROOSEVELT HICKS	James A. Williams
STERLING JOHNSON	John Earl Jelks
ELDER JOSEPH BARLOW	Anthony Chisholm

The play was produced on July 31, 2005, at the Center Theatre Group/Mark Taper Forum (Gordon Davidson, Founding Artistic Director; Michael Ritchie, Artistic Director; Charles Dillingham, Managing Director) in Los Angeles. It was directed by Kenny Leon; the set design was by David Gallo, the costume design was by Susan Hilferty, the lighting design was by Donald Holder, the sound design was by Jon Gottlieb, original music was composed and arranged by Kathryn Bostic; the production stage managers were Narda E. Alcorn and Mary K Klinger, and the dramaturg was Todd Kreidler. The cast was as follows:

HARMOND WILKS	Rocky Carroll
MAME WILKS	Denise Burse
ROOSEVELT HICKS	James A. Williams
STERLING JOHNSON	John Earl Jelks
ELDER JOSEPH BARLOW	Anthony Chisholm

The play was produced on January 25, 2006, at Seattle Repertory Theatre (David Esbjornson, Artistic Director; Benjamin Moore, Managing Director) in Seattle. It was directed by Kenny Leon; the set design was by David Gallo, the costume design was by Susan Hilferty, the lighting design was by Donald Holder, the sound design was by Dominic Cody Kramers, original music was composed and arranged by Kathryn Bostic; the production stage manager was Narda E. Alcorn and the dramaturg was Todd Kreidler. The cast was as follows:

HARMOND WILKS	Rocky Carroll
MAME WILKS	Denise Burse
ROOSEVELT HICKS	James A. Williams
STERLING JOHNSON	John Earl Jelks
ELDER JOSEPH BARLOW	Anthony Chisholm

The play was produced on March 29, 2006, at CENTER-STAGE (Irene Lewis, Artistic Director; Michael Ross, Managing Director) in Baltimore. It was directed by Kenny Leon; the set design was by David Gallo, the costume design was by Susan Hilferty, the lighting design was by Donald Holder, the sound design was by Amy C. Wedel, original music was composed by Kathryn Bostic; the stage manager was Marion Friedman and the dramaturg was Todd Kreidler. The cast was as follows:

HARMOND WILKS	Rocky Carroll
MAME WILKS	Denise Burse

ROOSEVELT HICKS	James A. Williams
STERLING JOHNSON	John Earl Jelks
ELDER JOSEPH BARLOW	Anthony Chisholm

The play was produced on September 13, 2006, at the Huntington Theatre Company (Nicholas Martin, Artistic Director; Michael Maso, Managing Director) in Boston. It was directed by Kenny Leon; the set design was by David Gallo, the costume design was by Susan Hilferty, the lighting design was by Donald Holder, the sound design was by Dan Moses Schreier, original music was composed by Kathryn Bostic; the production stage manager was Marion Friedman, the stage manager was Eileen Ryan Kelly and the dramaturg was Todd Kreidler. The cast was as follows:

HARMOND WILKS	Hassan El-Amin
MAME WILKS	Michole Briana White
ROOSEVELT HICKS	James A. Williams
STERLING JOHNSON	Eugene Lee
ELDER JOSEPH BARLOW	Anthony Chisholm

The play was produced on January 13, 2007, at The Goodman Theatre (Robert Falls, Artistic Director; Roche Schulfer, Executive Director) in Chicago. It was directed by Kenny Leon; the set design was by David Gallo, the costume design was by Susan Hilferty, the lighting design was by Donald Holder, the sound design was by Dan Moses Schreier, original music was composed by Kathryn Bostic, the production stage managers were Narda E. Alcorn and Marion Friedman, the stage manager was Joseph Drummond and the dramaturg was Todd Kreidler. The cast was as follows:

HARMOND WILKS	Hassan El-Amin
MAME WILKS	Michole Briana White

ROOSEVELT HICKS	James A. Williams
STERLING JOHNSON	John Earl Jelks
ELDER JOSEPH BARLOW	Anthony Chisholm

The play was produced on March 18, 2007, at the McCarter Theatre Center (Emily Mann, Artistic Director; Jeffrey Woodward, Managing Director) in Princeton, New Jersey. It was directed by Kenny Leon; the set design was by David Gallo, the costume design was by Susan Hilferty, the lighting design was by Donald Holder, original music and sound design were by Dan Moses Schreier; the production stage manager was Narda E. Alcorn, the stage manager was Marion Friedman and the dramaturg was Todd Kreidler. The cast was as follows:

HARMOND WILKS	Harry Lennix
MAME WILKS	Tonya Pinkins
ROOSEVELT HICKS	James A. Williams
STERLING JOHNSON	John Earl Jelks
ELDER JOSEPH BARLOW	Anthony Chisholm

On April 20, 2007, *Radio Golf* opened at the Cort Theatre on Broadway. It was directed by Kenny Leon; the set design was by David Gallo, the costume design was by Susan Hilferty, the lighting design was by Donald Holder, original music was composed and arranged by Dan Moses Schreier; the production stage manager was Narda E. Alcorn, the stage manager was Marion Friedman and the dramaturg was Todd Kreidler. The cast was as follows:

HARMOND WILKS	Harry Lennix
MAME WILKS	Tonya Pinkins
ROOSEVELT HICKS	James A. Williams
STERLING JOHNSON	John Earl Jelks
ELDER JOSEPH BARLOW	Anthony Chisholm

ACT ONE

The lights come up on the office of Bedford Hills Redevelopment, Inc. There are unpacked boxes scattered about. Mame Wilks enters and takes in the office. Harmond Wilks enters with his arms full of boxes.

MAME: This is it? This isn't anything like the way you described it. This ceiling's what you were so excited about?

HARMOND: Look close. See the embossing on the tin.

MAME: Harmond, it looks raggedy.

HARMOND: See those marks. It's all hand tooled. That's the only way you get pattern detail like that. That tin ceiling's worth some money.

MAME: Then take it down and sell it. At least put some new paint on it. I wouldn't want to do business here.

HARMOND: This is a construction office. It's not to impress anybody.

MAME: Your campaign office cannot look like this.

HARMOND: I'm going to put the campaign office in Reese's old wallpaper and paint store up on the corner of Centre and Kirkpatrick. It's got a lot of windows. People can see inside.

MAME: We decided to open your office in Shadyside. What's wrong with Shadyside? Right there on Ellsworth where that old bookstore used to be. That's got a lot of windows too. What's wrong with Shadyside?

HARMOND: I'm from the Hill District.

MAME: The population of the Hill isn't but thirty-five hundred people. And it's hard to get them to vote.

HARMOND: You don't understand. Politics is about symbolism. Black people don't vote but they have symbolic weight.

MAME: That's what Thomas Brown said when he ran for mayor. You see what he's doing now. Fixing parking tickets.

HARMOND: I have a plan. Thomas Brown didn't have a plan.

MAME: I have a plan too. My plan has your campaign office sitting in Shadyside. You don't want to start out your campaign excluding people. And how am I supposed to get the TV trucks to come up to the Hill? They won't drive up here until there's been a shooting.

HARMOND: This is what puzzles me. You have every step planned out for what I have to do to be mayor but when we do something simple like go out to dinner, you can't make up your mind what to eat. Then whatever I order is what you end up eating.

MAME: I need that copy of your speech to get to the *Post-Gazette*. They're anxious to publish it but they need it by Wednesday. They want to run it in Sunday's paper. And they need to take a photo of you on Tuesday.

HARMOND: I'll check my schedule with Dena.

MAME: I already spoke with her. You're free at eleven.

(Roosevelt Hicks enters. He carries an artist's rendering of their redevelopment project on foam board.)

ROOSEVELT: Where'd you park at?

HARMOND: There's a lot next door.

ROOSEVELT: Naw. Naw. I got to *see* my car. These niggers be done stole the hubcaps.

HARMOND: What hubcaps? You don't have any hubcaps. They quit making hubcaps in 1962.

ROOSEVELT: That's what I'm saying. They'll get mad there aren't any hubcaps and steal the wheels. One man asked me for five dollars. I told him I'd give him five dollars if he watched my car. He want to know how long I was gonna be. Like he got something to do. He's just lazy. Ain't got to do nothing but stand there and keep the rest of the niggers from stealing my tires and my radio. He worried about how long I'm going to be.

HARMOND: Park in the lot and you won't have any problem.

ROOSEVELT: I can't *see* the lot from here. I told you I got to watch my car.

MAME: Morning, Roosevelt.

ROOSEVELT: Hey, Mame. You heard anything from the governor yet?

MAME: I told his office I wasn't available until after our campaign. I don't want them to think I'm too available. If they find out I'm too excited about that job they'll determine I must not be qualified.

ROOSEVELT: The governor's press representative.
    Wait till you see this. (*Reveals the rendering*) I just picked it up from the architect.

MAME: Where's the Starbucks? Don't tell me they're going to put it inside the Barnes & Noble.

ROOSEVELT: No. It's right there on the other side of Whole Foods.

MAME: That apartment building turned out nice. Putting the garden on the roof really works.

ROOSEVELT: That was a good idea you had.

MAME: I saw it in a magazine.

ROOSEVELT: It's still a good idea. I don't care if it was in a magazine.

HARMOND: What's that? Why is it still called Model Cities Health Center?

MAME: Our board hasn't voted yet. We vote on the name change next meeting.

HARMOND: I've talked with most of the board members. I know their vote. They're going to change the name.

MAME: I'm voting it should stay Model Cities Health Center.

HARMOND: Sarah Degree was the first black registered nurse in the city. Naming it after her fits perfectly.

MAME: Model Cities Health Center has been around for twenty-two years. The organization has some history in the neighborhood. Nobody knows who Sarah Degree was.

HARMOND: That's why the Health Center needs to be named after her. So we remember.

MAME: I mean that's nice and I understand the sentiment but it's just not practical to throw all that history away.

(Roosevelt puts up a poster of Tiger Woods on the wall. Harmond picks up the phone on the desk.)

HARMOND: Hey Dena, Harmond here. I need you to get me into the Health Center's next board meeting. Get me in to speak with the board before they vote on the name change. Move whatever you need to in the schedule. (Pause) Yeah . . . Roosevelt just brought the rendering but call and tell them we need a new one. Have it say "Sarah Degree Health Center" instead of "Model Cities." (Pause) No, that's it. (Pause) I don't know the number yet. Wait a minute . . . (Rummages around on the desk until he finds it) 391-7795. Thanks. (Hangs up)

ROOSEVELT: How much you think Tiger makes a swing? I wish Nike would buy a piece of me.

MAME: Harmond, I need that copy of your speech.

ROOSEVELT: What's this I hear about them putting your speech in the paper?

MAME: I got the *Post-Gazette* to run it on Sunday. They're taking his picture too.

ROOSEVELT: That's all they're talking about down at the bank.

MAME: After his speech, some woman who goes to the annual breakfast meeting of the chamber of commerce every year said to me that Harmond was the first invited speaker who actually had an idea about developing city commerce.

ROOSEVELT: All I want to know is . . . when you become mayor can I get an office right next to yours? Make me some kind of advisor or something. I wouldn't mind having an office in Mellon Bank and at City Hall.

HARMOND (*Handing Mame a copy of the speech*): Make sure they get your approval if they want to edit anything.

MAME: Of course I will. (*Looks at her watch*) Oh . . . I got to go. I have to go over to Three Rivers. I'm covering a big photo shoot of Al Frank for *Sports Illustrated*.

ROOSEVELT: See if you can get me an autographed bat.

MAME: Harmond, don't forget we're going to Marcie and Jim's tonight. Six o'clock.

HARMOND: Remind me to take Jim one of those Cohibas I got in Costa Rica. I haven't smoked any of them yet.

MAME: I hope for you it stays warm out tonight. Marcie's not going to let you stink up her house either.

(*Mame exits. Harmond holds the rendering.*)

HARMOND: I don't know how "Model Cities" got on there. It should say "Sarah Degree Health Center."

ROOSEVELT: It's not going to say anything if the city doesn't declare the Hill District blighted. How are we going to do this if we don't get the fed money?

HARMOND: What are you worried for? The feds are ready to fund the project. And the city's not going to mess that up.

They're not going to pass up five million dollars even if it is for minority redevelopment. They're going to declare it blighted.

ROOSEVELT: We're out two hundred thousand dollars ourselves if they don't. That's real money out of our pockets. We paid the architect fee, contractor's holding fee, surveyor's fee, the demolition fee. It cost five thousand dollars just for the building permits. That's coming out of our pockets. This shit should have been taken care of months ago.

HARMOND: You know it takes six months to get a street light replaced.

ROOSEVELT: If the blight don't come through in six months the bank will have the keys to my house and Arleen's new Saab. I'll have to drive Arleen to work and rent a house from you. They'll have to fight me over my Lexus. I can't afford six months like you.

HARMOND: City council has to go through all that bureaucracy. But the blight will come through. Any fool can look around here and see that the Hill District's not fit to live in. Herm's on top of it.

ROOSEVELT: He's not but so much on top of it. The other city councilmen still want to shake Gordy's hand. It's him that's holding it up. Gordy with his do-nothing ass. When the newspapers started calling him "Do-Nothing Gordy" that's the only time they ever got anything right.

HARMOND: Everybody knows the Democratic Party's looking to dump Gordy. When I announce my candidacy at the groundbreaking ceremony next month you'll feel the ground shift and the wind will start blowing our way. Once the Party's behind me, all the city council will be in line to shake *my* hand. See how fast the Hill District's declared blighted then.

ROOSEVELT: I'll trust you on that. Just don't forget about getting me my office.

(He notices a trophy on Harmond's desk and picks it up.)

I see you still got Raymond's trophy. I remember you had that in our room at school. I'm sorry I never met him.

HARMOND: How's the golf camp going?

ROOSEVELT: I signed up two more kids last week. That makes eighteen. I just want these kids to know what it feels like to hit a golf ball. I hit my first golf ball I asked myself where have I been? How'd I miss this? I couldn't believe it. I felt free. Truly free. For the first time. I watched the ball soar down the driving range. I didn't think it could go so high. It just kept going higher and higher. I felt something lift off of me. Some weight I was carrying around and didn't know it. I felt like the world was open to me. Everything and everybody. I never did feel exactly like that anymore. I must have hit a hundred golf balls trying to get that feeling. But that first time was worth everything. I felt like I had my dick in my hand and was waving it around like a club. "I'm a man! Anybody want some of this come and get it!" That was the best feeling of my life.

HARMOND: That's what gets you hooked.

ROOSEVELT: That's why I keep my golf clubs in the trunk of my car just in case I drive by a golf course. I keep looking for that feeling. That's what I want these kids to have. That'll give them a chance at life. I wish somebody had come along and taught me how to play golf when I was ten. That'll set you on a path to life where everything is open to you. You don't have to hide and crawl under a rock just 'cause you black. Feel like you don't belong in the world.

(Harmond's cell phone rings. He answers it.)

HARMOND: Hey, Mame. *(Pause)* What man? What house? *(Pause)* The house on the development site? *(Pause)* Yeah . . .

we'll do something about it. (*Pause*) Okay, thanks. Talk with you later. (*Hangs up*) That was Mame. She was driving by the site and saw a man painting that house.

ROOSEVELT: Why would somebody paint that old ugly house?

HARMOND: She said a man was painting it.

ROOSEVELT: There's a big sign on it says we're tearing it down the first of the month.

HARMOND: Maybe he can't read.

ROOSEVELT: That's the damnedest thing I heard. I'll walk up there and see what's going on.

HARMOND: Tell him not to waste his paint.

(*Roosevelt exits. Harmond stares at the walls. He picks up a poster of Martin Luther King, Jr., and hangs it on the wall. Sterling Johnson enters.*)

STERLING: I been waiting for this office to open a long time. I do construction work. I'm looking for a job. (*Recognizing Harmond*) Hey . . . Harmond Wilks. Remember me? Sterling Johnson. We used to go to Saint Richard's school together.

HARMOND: Sterling Johnson.

STERLING: Remember that time I punched you in the mouth? I was punching everybody in the mouth back then. It felt good. I was mad at everybody. I don't do that shit no more. You remember that?

HARMOND: Yeah, I remember.

STERLING: Why didn't you punch me back? It wasn't nothing but some fisticuffs. Raymond punched me back. Hey man, I was sorry to hear about Raymond. I felt like crying when I heard that. Somebody told me say, "Raymond Wilks got killed in Vietnam." That made me feel real bad. You remember me and Raymond used to play together? We used to play cowboys and Indians. Raymond didn't like to die. You say, "Bang! You dead." Raymond would say, "You missed." We used to argue over who was going to be the Indians. We used to take turns. Yeah, I miss Raymond. We was on the football team together. Didn't nobody throw a football like Raymond. He'd throw a perfect spiral every time. Raymond told me he was going to go to Grambling. I was looking for him to make it to the pros. Next thing I know somebody say he got killed in Vietnam. You didn't go to Vietnam, did you?

HARMOND: I was in school.

STERLING: I was in jail. You know I robbed a bank? I don't know if you know that?

HARMOND: Yeah, I heard.

STERLING: People think I'm dumb 'cause I robbed that bank. I just wanted to know what it was like to have some money. Seem like everybody else had some. I said let me get me some. So I robbed that bank. I had some money. It didn't make me smarter. It didn't make me better than anybody else. You can't do nothing with money but spend it. After that you back where you started from. Then what you gonna do? I found out I was looking for something that you couldn't spend. That seem like the better of the two. To me. Everybody got their own way of looking at it but if you ask me . . . I'd take something you couldn't spend over money any day.

HARMOND: You do construction work?

STERLING: Yeah, I got my own business. They say you fixing to build up around here. That make sense seeing as how your family is in the real-estate business. Say you gonna build a supermarket and put in some apartments on that site up on Wylie.

HARMOND: We're going to bring the Hill back. We're going to rename it Bedford Hills.

STERLING: How you gonna bring it back? It's dead. It take Jesus Christ to bring it back. What you mean is you gonna put something else in its place. Say that. But don't talk about bringing the Hill back. The Hill District's dead.

HARMOND: We're going to bring back the whole area. Get some houses and some stores and shops. We're going to rebuild the whole neighborhood. You say you do construction work?

STERLING: Yeah, I fix houses. I know how to do anything. Sometimes I got to borrow some tools but I know how to fix anything.

HARMOND: Where did you go to school? Did you go to Connelly Trade?

STERLING: I went down there and they told me they didn't have no openings. Asked me did I want a job in the cafeteria. I told them to kiss my ass. I didn't know what to do then. Mr. Jackson say, "Pick up that hammer and come on." Mr. Jackson was in the union. He taught me how to be a union man. He say, "You gonna learn, you may as well learn right."

HARMOND: Do you have a résumé?

STERLING: Go up on Bedford and look where I fixed that porch. I fixed up a house around on Webster. 1615. Go look at that. Almost everything you see fixed up around here I did it. I do good work. Go around to Bedford and look at that porch.

(Roosevelt enters.)

HARMOND: Hey, Roosevelt. This is Sterling Johnson. He does construction work.

ROOSEVELT: How you doing, my man? We could use someone like you. We can put you to work. We can make an opportunity for you. I know it's a hard world. It's hard for everybody. But if we stick together we can do it. We can use a man like you.

STERLING: How much you paying? I'm a union man.

ROOSEVELT: We pay union wages to qualified union members.

STERLING: When do I start?

HARMOND: We'll be getting things started soon. Do you have a number where we can call you?

STERLING: I got one this week. I don't know about next week. You got a pencil. I ain't got no pencil. 365-8216. You got that?

HARMOND: We'll give you a call, Sterling.

(*They shake hands.*)

STERLING: Call me before the phone company cut off my phone.

(*Sterling exits.*)

HARMOND: Was there anybody up there?

ROOSEVELT: Yeah, there was somebody up there.

HARMOND: What was he doing?

ROOSEVELT: He was painting the house.

HARMOND: What color?

ROOSEVELT: You think it's funny. I don't think it's funny. I think it's sad.

HARMOND: It is funny if you stop and think about it. Somebody actually painting an abandoned house. Did you tell him we owned that house?

ROOSEVELT: Yeah, I told him.

HARMOND: What he say?

ROOSEVELT: He say he didn't care. He kept on painting the house.

HARMOND: Who is he?

ROOSEVELT: Damned if I know. I couldn't get no sense out of him. He don't know how to answer a simple question like, "What's your name?" He'll make that complicated.

HARMOND: Why is he painting the house?

ROOSEVELT: He say it's his property. I told him that was our property and that it was slated to be torn down. That went right over his head. I asked him where his deed was, he say it's on record downtown.

HARMOND: That house has been abandoned for the past twelve years.

ROOSEVELT: I told him he was defacing private property and if he didn't stop I was going to have him put in jail. He told me to go to hell.

HARMOND: How did you leave it? Did he stop painting the house?

ROOSEVELT: When I left he was sitting down resting. Had the paintbrush in his hand. He say he gets tired quick. I told him I was gonna send the police to make him stop. He started laughing. Now you think anybody who had some sense would understand what that mean. That mean you going to jail. He laughed at me. I want to see if he'll be laughing when the police go by there.

HARMOND: The police will make him stop. Then he'll probably go paint somebody else's house.

ROOSEVELT: I have to run down the bank and pick up my new business cards. I got my promotion and don't have any cards. My boss told me he forgot to order them. They supposed to be ready this afternoon. I don't have no cards to pass out on the golf course. Without them cards they'll think I'm the caddie.

(*Roosevelt exits. The lights go down on the scene.*)

SCENE 2

The radio is on in the office: "This is WBTZ in Pittsburgh. Running at the hot end of your dial. Ouch! Don't touch it. It'll burn ya!" The lights come up on Harmond displaying the revised rendering. Elder Joseph Barlow enters.

OLD JOE: You know where I can find any Christian people?

HARMOND: Find who?

OLD JOE: Christian people. I'm looking for some Christian people.

HARMOND: They all over. Look around. Everybody you bump into is probably a Christian.

OLD JOE: I can't find any. They told me to go to the Mission. I went out there and the missionaries were drilling holes in cups. If you broke one of their rules they'd drill a hole in your cup so the coffee run out the bottom. They had a couple men standing around trying to plug up that hole with their finger. I say I'm in the wrong place.

     You don't mind if I sit, do you?

HARMOND: No, go ahead. What can I do for you?

OLD JOE (*Sitting*): My dog died.

HARMOND: I'm sorry to hear that.

OLD JOE: Cost me three hundred dollars to bury her. Three hundred dollars for a dog! Used to be you could bury anybody for three hundred dollars. Don't care if he was the doctor or the president. Three hundred dollars would put *anybody* in the ground. They told me to call the dog pound. Say they would take her away for free. I figure she done served two masters she deserve a decent funeral.

HARMOND: You did the right thing. A dog is honest company. A dog doesn't pass judgment. A dog will stick with you no matter who you are. As long as you feed it.

OLD JOE: That was eight years ago. April 4, 1989. I ain't forgot about her.

HARMOND: I got a lot of work to do here. I got a stack of bids to go through.

OLD JOE: Are you a lawyer? I need a lawyer. I'd go see the gypsy if I knew where to find one.

HARMOND: This is a redevelopment office. You have to go down to Hill House. They'll help you get a lawyer down there.

OLD JOE: Somebody sent me by here. Say you was a big man. I always wanted to be a big man like you.

HARMOND: I ain't a big man. I'm going to run for mayor. If I win I'll be a big man.

OLD JOE: They ain't gonna let no black man be the mayor. Got too many keys. The mayor got more keys than the janitor. They ain't gonna let you have that many keys.

HARMOND: Look . . . If you want a lawyer go down to Hill House. Tell them I sent you. Tell them Harmond Wilks sent you.

OLD JOE: I know you. You one of the Wilks brothers. I knew your daddy and I knew your brother. You had a brother named Raymond. A twin brother. Everybody know the Wilks Twins. Harmond and Raymond Wilks. You probably got places to go and people to see. That's what I told my mama when I left home. And I been some places and I seen some people. I seen Muhammad Ali. In Louisville, March 5, 1978. I left Nashville with forty-six dollars and eighty-four cents. And ended up in Louisville with a hundred and sixty-eight dollars. I ain't gonna tell you how that happened. I thought I was a rich man. That was like a perfect day. A perfect day is the saddest day. You know why? 'Cause it has to come to an end. I've had many perfect days. I thought they were going to last forever. But they all come to an end. The only problem is you never know if you're going to have another one. I had a nice little old ride on that hundred and sixty-eight dollars till I ended up broke and in the poorhouse. I been in the poorhouse ever since. You got green money but I never did turn my money green. That's just the way it turned out but it could have turned out another way. You sure you ain't a lawyer? I need a lawyer like you. We got a nice rapport.

HARMOND: What you need a lawyer for? They have some good lawyers down at Hill House.

OLD JOE: They had me charged with fraud. Tried to put me in jail.

HARMOND: Fraud? What did you do?

OLD JOE: I didn't do nothing but walk the dog.

HARMOND: Naw . . . naw. They weren't going to put you in jail for walking a dog. Why were they going to put you in jail for fraud?

OLD JOE: 'Cause Mr. Douglas died. Mr. Douglas was a blind man. He lived downstairs from me. He had a dog named Cindy. When he died Cindy ain't had nothing to do so I let her lead me around just so she be happy. They tried to put me in jail for being a fake blind man. I didn't do nothing but walk the dog. I will tell the truth though. The sun was shining so I did put on some sunglasses.

HARMOND: Did you solicit money from anybody?

OLD JOE: That's a ten-dollar word with a five-dollar meaning. I ain't never asked nobody for nothing. But the people give me all the time. They don't want to see me want for nothing. They been giving me for years. I used to go around singing songs and the people like that. They take care of me. If I had my guitar I'd sing one for you. But my guitar's in the pawnshop. It's been in the pawnshop since January 22, 1970.

HARMOND: I can't help you. You have to go down to Hill House.

OLD JOE: Is you really running for mayor? They ain't gonna let you be mayor.

HARMOND: This is 1997. Things have changed. This is America. This is the land of opportunity. I can be mayor. I can be anything I want.

OLD JOE: But you got to have the right quarter. America is a giant slot machine. You walk up and put in your coin and it spits it back out. You look at your coin. You think maybe it's a Canadian quarter. It's the only coin you got. If this coin ain't no good then you out of luck. You look at it and sure enough it's an American quarter. But it don't spend for you. It spend for everybody else but it don't spend for you. The machine spits it right back out. Is the problem with the quarter or with the machine? Do you know? Somebody running for mayor ought to know that.

HARMOND: If it don't take all the quarters you fix it. Anybody with common sense will agree to that. What they don't agree on is how to fix it. Some people say you got to tear it down to fix it. Some people say you got to build it up to fix it. Some people say they don't know how to fix it. Some people say they don't want to be bothered with fixing it. You mix them all in a pot and stir it up and you got America. That's what makes this country great.

OLD JOE: I say get a new machine. What you say?

HARMOND: We fixing it. We're going to redevelop this whole area. We'll get the Hill District growing so fast people from all over will start moving back.

OLD JOE: If you do win mayor they gonna change the rules and only give you half the keys. You know that, don't you?

HARMOND: Naw, I'm going to have all the keys and they're going to have to make me some new ones. We are going to build up everything. Look at this. (*Shows Old Joe the rendering*) We finally get a supermarket in the Hill District. New apartments. The Sarah Degree Health Center. Do you know Sarah Degree was the first black registered nurse in Pittsburgh? This is just the beginning.

OLD JOE: You gonna put some lights up on Kennard Field?

HARMOND: We're going to put a golf driving range up there. Make it part of the CitiParks project.

OLD JOE: You need some lights. Kennard Field's the only football field in the city ain't got no lights. The city say they ran out of electricity. That's what they say in 1952. I could still run up and down the field then. You gonna put some lights up there?

HARMOND: You don't need any lights. All the parks close at dusk.

OLD JOE: See? You ain't even got to be mayor and you acting like one. The first word come out your mouth is "no." The people been waiting fifty years for some lights. Why can't we have some lights? Everybody else got them. They had some kids go blind playing up there at night without no lights. They started going blind in 1959. The people been trying to get some lights up there since 1952 and they ain't got them yet. I'm gonna die and they still ain't gonna have no lights up there.

HARMOND: There's nobody using that field now except for a few kids.

OLD JOE: That's what I'm saying . . . they don't want to go blind. If you put some lights up there the people will come. They ain't gonna come for nothing. But you put some lights up there and watch the people come from all over. They'll come dancing. They gonna throw a big party. You put some lights up there and the people will hang a picture of you in their living room.

HARMOND: You teach the kids how to play golf and they have all the rules they need to win at life. You ever play golf?

OLD JOE: Don't you need some grass? Ain't no grass around here. Archie had a golf club. He used to carry it around in case somebody messed with him. That's the only time I ever seen a golf club. I asked myself then what good was it? Time Archie draw back to hit somebody they be done stabbed him five times.

HARMOND: Look here, I got to get back to work.

OLD JOE: Is you gonna be my lawyer? I need a lawyer like you.

HARMOND: How come you don't want to go to Hill House? You got something against the lawyers down there?

OLD JOE: I hate to go down there. They tell you, "Sit over there and wait." "Fill out this paper." "Turn over." "Jump up and down." I tried to tell them I wasn't no dog but they wasn't listening. Told me to go down to the Animal Rescue Society if I wanted a license for my dog. I told them I wanted to see a lawyer. They told me, "Fill out this form." "Sit down over there and wait." "Turn over." "Jump up and down."

(Roosevelt enters.)

ROOSEVELT *(To Old Joe)*: What you doing here?

OLD JOE: I'm talking to this gentleman right here. He's my
lawyer.

ROOSEVELT: You should be in jail. Defacing private property.
You're going to need two lawyers. Harmond, this is the
man who was painting the house. Try and get some sense
out of him.

HARMOND: You were painting our house up on Wylie? Why
were you painting our house?

OLD JOE: My daughter say she wanna live there. I was fixing it
up for her.

ROOSEVELT: I told you we're tearing down that house. That's
abandoned property. That house belongs to Bedford Hills
Redevelopment.

OLD JOE: That's my house. I got the deed on record down at
the courthouse. My mother put it down there in 1925.

ROOSEVELT: You going to jail. They got a senior citizen jail
near Harrisburg. That's where you heading. Defacing private property. What the police tell you?

OLD JOE: They say, "How you doing, sir? If anybody mess with
you . . . you just call us, sir. We here to serve and protect,
sir." That's what it say on their cars: "Serve and Protect."
They must have thought I was a white man.

ROOSEVELT: See what I'm talking about, Harmond? What's
your name?

OLD JOE: I'll take the Fifth Amendment. I know my rights.

ROOSEVELT: But do you know your name? That's the question.

OLD JOE: I don't know yours. If I knew yours maybe I'd tell
you mine. Then we'd be even.

ROOSEVELT: My name is Roosevelt Hicks.

OLD JOE: Pleased to meet you.

ROOSEVELT: What's your name?

OLD JOE: I ain't got to tell you. If you was the police I'd have to tell you. I know my rights. If my lawyer ask me I'd tell him. But I ain't got to tell you nothing.

HARMOND: What's your name?

ROOSEVELT: Harmond, you can't get no sense out of him.

OLD JOE: My name is Elder Joseph Barlow, but the people call me Old Joe. They been calling me that since I was ten. My mama called me Old Black Joe but I don't let nobody else call me that. I ain't never ran into anybody that special.

HARMOND: What did the police tell you?

OLD JOE: They say they was gonna charge me with vandalism for painting my own house. They gave me this. *(Hands Harmond a complaint summons)* That's why I come by here to get me a lawyer. Is you a Christian? If you was a Christian I figure you would see that I was falsely accused like Jesus Christ and maybe you wouldn't charge me as much. I can't pay but so much anyhow. Don't care how much you charge. But if you only charge a little maybe I can pay you all of it. That way I won't be in debt.

HARMOND: Did you stop painting the house?

OLD JOE: Yes, sir, I stopped painting it. That's a lot of work and I get tired easy. The policeman told me to stop and I stopped.

HARMOND: I'll call down and see if I can get this summons dismissed. *(Picks up the phone and dials)* Sergeant Griffin, please. *(Pause)* Harmond Wilks. *(Pause)* Hey Jimmy . . . *(Pause)* Thanks . . . thanks a lot. They're going to run the whole speech in the *Post-Gazette* on Sunday. *(Pause)* Yeah, I'm looking forward to it. Listen, I need to get a summons complaint dismissed on a man who was painting the house on our site at 1839 Wylie. *(Pause)* A misdemeanor summons. Number 201E6594. *(Pause)* Elder Joseph Barlow. *(Pause)* Yeah . . . Thanks, Jimmy. I appreciate it. *(Hangs up)*

(*Harmond tears up the summons.*)

OLD JOE: I knew you was a big man. But what I'm gonna tell my daughter? She say she wants to move back in my house.

HARMOND: Tell her she has to move somewhere else. She should be able to find a place. Have her go up to Wilks Realty on Centre and Herron and tell them I sent her.

OLD JOE: Everybody know Wilks Realty. Right up on the corner there. I used to know your daddy. I ain't gonna say nothing about him. My mama told me if you can't say something nice about somebody don't say nothing. Your daddy was a big man like you. He didn't have no truck with the little man. He always drew a line like that. He put the little man on one side and the big man on the other. My mama say everybody on the bed or everybody on the floor.

HARMOND: Look here, Mr. Barlow . . .

OLD JOE: You can call me Old Joe.

HARMOND: Look here, Old Joe.

OLD JOE: What do I call you?

HARMOND: You can call me Harmond.

OLD JOE: I remember you when you was a boy. Used to see you riding in the car eating ice cream. Everybody else was walking.

HARMOND: Look here, Old Joe. I called down and had the summons dismissed. If you still feel you need a lawyer go down to Hill House. Your daughter will have to find someplace else to live other than the house that we own.

OLD JOE: What about my deed? It's got my name on it.

(*Roosevelt tears through some files to find the demolition order. He hands it to Old Joe.*)

ROOSEVELT: The property at 1839 Wylie is owned by Bedford Hills Redevelopment and is slated to be torn down the first of the month. Can you read? This is a demolition order. It say it right there. Anybody painting it is trespassing and defacing private property.

OLD JOE: You act like you a rooster. You the King of the Barnyard. You strut through the barnyard during the day. At night you roost high up on the rafters. But when you get to the bottom of it a rooster ain't nothing but a chicken.

ROOSEVELT: Hey look, old man. You don't own the house anymore. That's what the man is trying to tell you. That can't be that hard to understand.

OLD JOE: I got my deed on record at the courthouse!

ROOSEVELT: Well, go down there and get it! See what they tell you. They'll tell you the same thing we telling you. We busy here. We got work to do. Go on down the courthouse and tell them down there.

(Roosevelt goes to the door and holds it open.)

OLD JOE: My mama taught me manners if she ain't taught me nothing else. You supposed to say, "Have a good day."

ROOSEVELT: Go on now, we're busy.

(Old Joe exits.)

I don't know how you put up with him. I ain't got no patience for that kind of shit. The man is crazy. I don't understand why you called and had the summons dismissed.

HARMOND: The man hasn't done anything but waste his paint. Come the first of the month it'll be a pile of bricks.

ROOSEVELT: Hey, Harmond. Guess what? I got a call from Bernie Smith. Invited me in on a round. Wants me to complete his foursome on Friday.

HARMOND: What does he want?

ROOSEVELT: Who cares? This is Bernie Smith. Whatever it is means some money. Bernie Smith don't play golf with just anybody. He play with millionaires. I ain't there yet but playing golf with people like Bernie Smith will get me there.

HARMOND: Do you read the newspaper? The fallout over that Duquesne Light deal just hit. Bernie Smith's got seventeen people suing him.

ROOSEVELT: If he's got that many people suing him must mean the man's making some money.

HARMOND: Watch yourself.

(Roosevelt takes out his business card.)

ROOSEVELT: Look at this.

HARMOND *(Reads)*: "Roosevelt Hicks. Vice President. Mellon Bank." Man, this is long overdue. Now you can afford to take me out to lunch.

ROOSEVELT: That's the second card I gave out. I gave the first one to John Albrecht so he won't forget I'm a Vice President at Mellon Bank. He's still pissed it came from above him that he had to promote me. He had somebody else in mind. Wait till Bernie Smith sees that. This is the big time. Nothing but blue skies. *(Singing:)*

> Blue skies smiling at me
> Nothing but blue skies do I see
>
> Never saw the sun shining so bright
> Never saw things going so right.

(Roosevelt suddenly notices something out the window and bolts for the door.)

Hey! Hey! Get off my car!

(The lights go down on the scene.)

SCENE 3

The lights come up on Harmond and Mame in the office.

HARMOND: You can't cut that. How can you cut that from my speech?

MAME: I thought you wanted to be mayor, Harmond.

HARMOND: I'll call the *Post-Gazette* myself. It goes back in.

MAME: You want to be mayor you better start acting like one.

HARMOND: They can print the whole speech or nothing at all. This is bullshit.

MAME: I'm not wasting my time on your campaign if you're not committed to winning this. I'm sacrificing my business. Giving up my clients. Harmond, we've worked too hard.

HARMOND: I'm not running to be the police commissioner's mayor.

MAME: We need him at the groundbreaking ceremony. Do you understand how important this is? If the commissioner doesn't come, we throw away our police support. Then we lose the firemen and the labor unions will start to worry. Who wants a mayor who can't protect the city? Commissioner Bell needs to be at the groundbreaking and you're going to have to play it. Smile. Shake hands. Let the commissioner get his picture with you holding the silver shovel.

HARMOND: I won't—under any circumstances—take back what I said.

MAME: You don't have to take it back. Just keep it out of the paper. Right now we don't need it in print. After we get you elected, then you can say all that stuff.

HARMOND: Stuff? What stuff? All you're hearing is *stuff*? An innocent man gets shot by the police and the officer gets away with it and he gets a promotion?

MAME: That was three years ago, Harmond. All the people hear is, "Oh, that guy's still harping on that. He needs to quit complaining."

HARMOND: Is the man still dead? Is the officer who killed him still getting a raise and Christmas bonus every year? And a goddamn turkey to boot!

MAME: Nobody's going to vote for an angry mayor.

HARMOND: Yeah, I'm angry! Aren't you? I care about this city. It's almost bankrupt. It's ill managed. The infrastructure is falling apart. Everything's ground down by bureaucratic bullshit. The whole goddamn city should be angry. We got a do-nothing mayor who's beholden to the money interests. Probably can't even name his department heads.

MAME: Everybody knows that. Everybody's angry—

(Old Joe enters.)

OLD JOE: That's a nice car you got out there in the lot. How many miles you got on it? I bet these shoes got more miles on them. That gold-on-black lettering's nice too. Good thing they didn't scratch it when they broke in your trunk.

(Harmond starts for the door.)

HARMOND: Goddamn . . .

(Harmond exits.)

OLD JOE: It took me fourteen minutes. I used to be able to walk from downtown in six minutes. You got to come up that hill. If I had me some PF Flyers I could make it in ten.

MAME: Is there something I can do for you?

OLD JOE: I'm looking for some Christian people. I went out to the Mission. Ain't no Christian people out there.

MAME: Mr. Wilks is very busy now. Can you come back later?

OLD JOE: I can wait. He's my lawyer. *(Sits)* They supposed to have some Christians out at the Mission but they forgot how to call on God. I seen the people call God down.

They don't do that too much no more. But I seen it happen. Over on the Northside. The fourteenth day of November 1937. The people called him down and God came in a blaze of glory. I seen him. Had a pot of water say he could make it boil without fire. The people wanna bet against God. You can't bet against God and win. The people put up their money. God walked over and stuck his hand in the pot and stirred it around. Told one of the fellows, "Now you do it." Man walked over and tried to stick his hand in the pot and had to draw it back. The pot was boiling! If you had thrown some beans in there you could have cooked your supper. He asked the people if they wondered how he could do that. He said, "I am He." He didn't say he was God. He just say, "I am He." But who else could he have been. Made a pot boil without fire. Can you do it? If you can't do it you ain't got nothing to say.

MAME: You say the people put up their money? They were betting against God? Well, tell me, did God walk out the door with the money? If God walked out the door with the money he wasn't nothing but a Negro from Mississippi with some dry ice.

(For the first time, Old Joe is speechless. After a beat, Harmond enters.)

Did they take anything? I told you to get a new alarm.

HARMOND: They got my clubs.

MAME: Thank God they didn't take the car.

HARMOND: I'd rather they took the car and left the clubs. You can always get a new car.

MAME: Our homeowners insurance will cover your clubs.

HARMOND: You can't replace them. They're a part of me. I got those clubs when I started playing golf twelve years ago. Right before taxes when I needed to spend some money before the government took it.

MAME: Should we call the police?

HARMOND: Why?

MAME: You need their report to file the insurance claim. Is the car damaged any?

HARMOND: Only the lock. They popped it off clean. We don't need to file an insurance claim. I'll take it over to the shop and get the lock replaced.

(Mame starts to leave.)

MAME: Think over what we talked about. You only got one shot at this, Harmond.

(Harmond picks up the phone and dials.)

HARMOND: Dena, Harmond here. Listen, call the *Post-Gazette*. Let them know they have to publish my speech in its entirety or not at all. (*Pause*) I don't know what their deadline is. I don't care. Call them now. (*Hangs up*)

(Mame, disappointed, stares at Harmond a beat before she exits.)

OLD JOE: I don't let no one woman rule my mind. It take six or seven. One cause too much trouble. One want everything. Them six or seven be happy with what they can get. It took me a while to learn that. It took me a while to learn a lot of things but I'm learning just the same. Is you learning anything? When your way get dark turn your lights up high. That's such a simple thing most people forget about it. They walk around in the dark complaining. You ever notice that?

HARMOND: You striking out in the dark and there's nobody there but yourself. You're all alone. I used to walk around in the dark complaining 'cause I couldn't find a woman.

I didn't understand. I had everything a woman could want. I had money, I had confidence, I was doing something with my life. They all used to tell me I was too intense. Too serious. That I needed to enjoy life. Shouldn't worry so much about the things I couldn't change. Then I met Mame. The first time I saw Mame it was raining. I thought she was gonna melt. The rain look like it hurt her. Like the two wasn't supposed to go together. You couldn't mix them up. That's what made her stand out. She had a frown on her face and the rain was beating on her. She hurt from the injustice of it. That's what made me like her. She could be strong and soft at the same time. I said I like that. I wished I had an umbrella but I didn't. I went and stood and blocked the rain. I told her she looked too pretty to be getting all wet. That's how we got talking. She called the rain some names I ain't gonna repeat.

(Harmond picks up the phone and dials.)

May I speak to Commissioner Bell please? *(Pause)* Harmond Wilks. *(Pause)* Can you tell the commissioner I called to invite him to the groundbreaking ceremony for the Bedford Hills Redevelopment site. It would mean a lot to me and to the community if the commissioner could be there. *(Pause)* Next month on the fourth, ten A.M. *(Pause)* I'll give you my office number. 391-7795. *(Pause)* Thank you. *(Hangs up)* Mr. Barlow, I already did what I could do for you. They dismissed your summons as long as you don't start painting the house again.

OLD JOE: I ain't painting the house. That was yesterday. Today's today. Tomorrow's been following me for a long time. Everywhere I go it follows me. It ain't caught me yet. Today's faster than tomorrow. Today I went down to see about my deed and they said you had it. Say you bought my house. That ain't but so bad. Only thing I didn't sell it. I tried to tell them that but they wasn't listening. They told me they sold it 'cause I owed back taxes.

HARMOND: How come you didn't pay the taxes?

OLD JOE: I didn't know I was supposed to pay them. My mother say we didn't pay no taxes.

HARMOND: Everybody has to pay taxes.

OLD JOE: My mother said she didn't pay none.

HARMOND: You know you have to pay taxes. The president has to pay taxes.

OLD JOE: The Barlow family didn't pay no taxes. Never did. Every time she went to pay them they was already paid.

HARMOND: Who was paying them then?

OLD JOE: I don't know. She didn't say that part. I don't know if she knew.

HARMOND: Anybody delinquent in their property taxes and abandons the property, the city can seize the property and sell it at a sheriff's auction.

OLD JOE: Don't they have to give me a notice or something? If you was gonna buy my house at least you'd think you'd tell me about it.

HARMOND: The notice of a sheriff's sale should've been posted in the paper.

OLD JOE: What am I gonna do?

HARMOND: There's nothing you can do. It's the law. The law protects you when you pay your taxes. But the law protects the city when a property's abandoned.

OLD JOE: But I didn't abandon the house. I'm right here. People act like I'm invisible. If somebody asks me I'll tell them I'm right here.

HARMOND: I don't know what to tell you other than your daughter will have to live somewhere else.

OLD JOE: Is this the kind of mayor you're gonna be? Just like your daddy. Put the big man on one side and the little man on the other.

HARMOND: Tell you what, Mr. Barlow. I'll look into this for you but I can't promise anything. This sounds like a straightforward case to me.

OLD JOE: How much you charge? I can't pay but a little bit.

HARMOND: You don't have to pay me anything.

OLD JOE: I got to pay you a little bit.

(Roosevelt enters dressed in his golf clothes. He is excited.)

ROOSEVELT: Hey Harmond, you should have seen it. I made two birdies on the back nine. I shot my best round ever. I couldn't believe it. The ball kept falling for me.

OLD JOE: Did I say I was leaving? I got to take care of some important business. I got places to go and people to see.

(Old Joe exits.)

ROOSEVELT: Bernie couldn't figure out what was happening. I told him next time we played I'd give him some strokes.

HARMOND: Did Bernie Smith pay your greens fee?

ROOSEVELT: Hell, Bernie paid the greens fee, paid for our caddies and picked up the tip. From the minute I set foot in Cedar Oaks Golf Course it was made clear my money was no good there. This is the big time.

HARMOND: How'd it go at the nineteenth hole? How many cards you pass out?

ROOSEVELT: I was the center of the table. Everybody buying me drinks 'cause of my game. The one guy was Australian, some kind of junk bond investor. And all I could get from the other guy was he must be independently wealthy. He plays golf twice a day. That's gonna be me one day.

HARMOND: Yeah, after you retire. If you can still walk.

ROOSEVELT: Naw, Harmond. It's gonna be much sooner than that.

AUGUST WILSON

(Roosevelt smiles like the cat who ate the canary.)

HARMOND: What? What happened? What are you talking about?

ROOSEVELT: I was the center of the table and the conversation was going as good as my game. There I was holding my own, breaking out ahead of the pack at a table of millionaires. Then I look up and it was just me and Bernie sitting there. Man to man. I thought to myself this is where I've been trying to get to my whole life. And then it happened. Bernie Smith wants to partner with me to buy WBTZ radio.

HARMOND: What? You're putting me on.

ROOSEVELT: Not only that but I'd be in charge. Bernie wants to be a silent partner. I call all the shots! I get to run day-to-day operations. I'm in charge of programming. Most important, I set the ad rates. My ship has come in.

HARMOND: But you don't know shit about radio.

ROOSEVELT: I know radio is the best advertising platform out there. You have no idea how much money's to be made in radio right now. Rates are sky-high and climbing every day.

HARMOND: Why's Bernie Smith want to partner with you? What's he get out of this?

ROOSEVELT: We get to buy the station for two-thirds of what it's worth. We buy it at an undervalued price and right out of the gate we're ahead making money.

HARMOND: That doesn't make any sense. Why would the owner of the station sell it undervalued? Is the station in debt?

ROOSEVELT: The owner gets a tax incentive. It's an advantage for him and an advantage for us.

HARMOND: Incentive for what? What do you bring to the table?

ROOSEVELT: The FCC offers a Minority Tax Certificate.

HARMOND: So you're the black face? You're just the front?

ROOSEVELT: Naw, Harmond. Naw. I get to get in the door. Remember in school we used to say we wanted to be in the

36

room when they count the money? You're there already. This is my shot.

HARMOND: You'll get in the room. All it takes is some time. You can't let Bernie Smith use you like this.

ROOSEVELT: This is how you do it! This is how everybody does it. You don't think Mellon has ever been used? We're talking about an eight-million-dollar radio station! This is the game! I'm at the table! There was a time they didn't let any blacks at the table. You opened the door. You shined the shoes. You served the drinks. And they went in the room and made the deal. I'm in the room! Them motherfuckers who bought and traded them railroads . . . how do you think they did it? This is business. This is the way it's done in America. I get to walk away with a piece of an asset worth eight million dollars. I don't care if somebody else makes some money 'cause of a tax break. I get mine and they get theirs. I pull this off and next time I'm on the other side of the deal, sitting at the head of the table. Right now I'm sitting here. I'd rather that than to be sitting on the other side of the door. Harmond, I have to take this. This is not going to come along again. The window of opportunity is already starting to close. If I don't do this Bernie will get somebody else.

HARMOND: All right, man. What lawyer are you going to use on the deal? You can't trust Bernie Smith.

ROOSEVELT: Bernie wanted to use *his* lawyer. I told him, "Naw, I got to bring in my own guy." I thought I'd use Scott. He did good work for us.

HARMOND: What's your percent of the station?

ROOSEVELT: He's offering ten, plus an annual percentage increase based on revenue not to exceed twenty-percent ownership. And I'll draw a salary for running the station.

HARMOND: You can't take the initial offer. Bernie Smith won't respect you if you do.

ROOSEVELT: I figured I'd ask for fifteen, take twelve and adjust my ownership allowance so it can accrue up to twenty-five percent. This is just the beginning, Harmond. I can set up a network. I know five or six stations to partner with. There's two in St. Louis. Newark. Atlanta. The door is wide open! All I got to do is walk through.

HARMOND: Just be careful.

ROOSEVELT: Remember what we used to say in school?

HARMOND AND ROOSEVELT (*Singing*):

> Hail! Hail! The gang's all here
> It's one for all, the big and small,
> It's always me for you.

(*They shake hands and embrace.*)

HARMOND: I got your back, man. I always got your back.

ROOSEVELT: Hey Harmond, I feel so good I could go for *another* round of golf. Come on, let's close the office. This round's on me. Let's go!

HARMOND: I can't.

ROOSEVELT: What do you mean you can't? You can't celebrate with me? This is the biggest day in my life!

HARMOND: My clubs got stolen out of my trunk.

ROOSEVELT (*Laughs*): I told you. That's why I got to *see* my car!

(*The lights go down on the scene.*)

SCENE 4

The lights come up on Harmond in the office. He is on the phone with a file in his hand.

HARMOND: You checked all the newspapers? (*Pause*) Do you have the right address? 1839 Wylie. (*Pause*) Dena, they had to have posted it in the paper at least thirty days before the auction. How far back did you go? *(Pause)* I have the deed right here. I'm sure it's the right date. I bought the house from the city on June 22, 1992. *(Pause)* It doesn't matter when I transferred ownership to Bedford Hills. That has nothing to do with the notice in the paper. *(Pause)* Why would you call Herm? *(Pause)* I have all those files here. Let me check.

(He puts down the phone and starts going through a file drawer. He pulls out a thick file and rifles through it. He stops when he sees one of the records.)

Shit. *(Returning to the phone)* Dena . . . never mind. Don't worry about it. I found out what happened. That's one of the houses I bought before it went to auction. *(Pause)* Don't call anybody about this yet. Let me figure out what to do. *(Pause)* Thanks. *(Hangs up)*

(He pulls some more papers out of the file and sets them aside on his desk, then puts the file away. Mame enters with her good news ready.)

Hey, sweets. I thought you were in meetings all day.

MAME: I got the job.

HARMOND: That's great! I'm so proud of you.

MAME: The governor just called me himself. Told me he had to find somebody qualified but instead got himself a superstar. There's still all the interview hoops to jump through but that's a formality. The governor told me after our campaign I can step right in.

HARMOND: Let's celebrate tonight. We can go to the Tin Angel.

MAME: Everything is lining up and going so good for us.

HARMOND: Why not forget about my campaign? Start your job soon as you can.

MAME: Your campaign? What campaign do you have without me?

HARMOND: I don't know. You always have the plan.

MAME: You just better hope you can follow it. Have you thought about the slogan yet? We can't sit on this any longer. If we don't move soon there won't be any buttons or anything to pass out at the groundbreaking. I still think we should go with: "Wilks Works for You."

HARMOND: What about: "Win with Wilks"?

MAME: That might work for a bumper sticker but we need something for the poster.

HARMOND: You can't really tell what will work till you see it.

(Mame takes out her yellow tablet and pages through her lists.)

MAME: I'll have some mock-ups made. Something we can look at. Do we still like: "Harmond Wilks: The People's Renaissance"?

HARMOND: People have heard "Renaissance" too many times in Pittsburgh. They hear that again and will think all I want to do is build shopping malls.

MAME: "This Is Your City"?

HARMOND: How about: "Now Is the Time"?

MAME: No, we don't need the "Now." Let's try: "It's Time." That works better. But my favorite's still: "Wilks Works for You." That will let the people know where you stand.

HARMOND: Those are good. Have them made up and we'll take a look at them.

MAME: What about colors?

HARMOND: I don't know. Try different colors. Let's see them.

MAME: Do you still want the flag on it?

HARMOND: That flag's most important. Don't hide it down in the corner or make it too small. Make sure it's waving high and strong, not hanging down looking defeated.

MAME: I'm going to have these slogans sent straight out to the designers. They can have something made up for us in the next couple of days. I feel so good about all this. Right

RADIO GOLF

here . . . this is where you get. Where hard work will take you.

(Sterling enters carrying a newspaper.)

STERLING: Harmond Wilks. Running for mayor! I heard that. I told myself it's about time. We need a black mayor. White folks had a hundred mayors in a row. I read your speech in the newspaper.

HARMOND: Sterling, this is my wife, Mame.

STERLING: Nice to meet you.

HARMOND: What do you think for my campaign slogan: "Wilks Works for You"?

STERLING: You know if you say that you gonna have to do it.

HARMOND: I mean every word I said in that speech. You can hold me to it.

STERLING: Say that: "Hold Me to It." Put that on your poster.

HARMOND: "Hold Me to It." That's a good one. Put that down too, Mame.

STERLING: I was gonna say: "By Any Means Necessary." But that ain't gonna work for you. Unless you want to be Malcolm X.

MAME: Let me go and get the designers started on these poster ideas. (To Sterling) Nice to meet you.

(Mame exits.)

STERLING (Reading from the newspaper): "The wealth of a city is not its two new stadiums. The wealth of a city is its people. People who need job opportunities that last longer than nine months of stadium building. People who need a city willing to invest in them with long-term jobs, enabling them to invest back in Pittsburgh the wealth of their work." We need them stadiums. Don't they hold big crowds of people? You're gonna need them. That's where

41

you're gonna have to put the unemployment office. You're gonna need both of them. "Police misconduct should never be rewarded. Everyone should be called into account for their actions. The police are public servants bound by an oath of duty to protect its citizenry by abiding and upholding the laws of the commonwealth. No one is above the law." Sound simple, don't it? "No one is above the law." You go downtown and try and tell them that. They act like they don't understand what you saying and then lock you up for being hostile.

HARMOND: Yeah, if I'm elected I'm going to change all that.

STERLING: I ain't here to interfere with your work. I just stopped by to check on the job.

HARMOND: When I called the union and tried to get you on the job they said you weren't a member.

STERLING: Naw . . . you don't understand. I'm my own union. I got my own everything. Except my own bank. But I got my own truck. I got my own tools. I got my own rules and I got my own union. I don't play no games. I have to have my own. That's the only way I got anything. I've been going through the back door all my life. See, people get confused about me. They did that ever since we was in school. But I know how to row the boat. I been on the water a long time. I know what it takes to plug the holes. I ain't dumb. Even though some people think I am. That give me an advantage. I found that out when I was in the orphanage. Mr. Redwood taught me that. He told me, "You ain't dumb, you just faster than everybody else." I was so fast it made me look slow. I was waiting for them to catch up . . . that made it look like I was standing around doing nothing. They kept me behind in the fourth grade 'cause I wouldn't add twelve and twelve. I thought it was stupid. Everybody know there's twelve to a dozen and twenty-four to two dozen. I don't care if it's donuts or oranges. They handed me the test and I turned it in blank.

If you had seventeen dollars and you bought a parrot for twelve dollars how many dollars would you have left? Who the hell gonna spend twelve dollars on a parrot? What you gonna do with it? Do you know how many chickens you can buy for twelve dollars? They thought I didn't know the answer. Every time somebody come to adopt me they say, "Well, Sterling's a little slow." That stuck with me. I started to believe it myself. Maybe they knew something I didn't know. That's when Mr. Redwood told me, "You ain't dumb. You just faster than everybody else." I've been going in the back doors all my life 'cause they don't never let me in the front.

(*Old Joe enters.*)

How you doing, Mr. Barlow?

OLD JOE: Nice job you did on that porch up on Bedford. You smell fried chicken? I smell fried chicken. They used to have a fried chicken place around the corner.

STERLING: Miss Harriet's.

HARMOND: How are you doing, Mr. Barlow?

OLD JOE: You can call me Old Joe. Miss Harriet had a fried chicken place right around the corner. Her and her two sisters. They had seven or eight kids between them and they would all get back in there and fry that chicken. I don't know what she did to it. But the people would line up for it.

STERLING: Saturday night the line would stretch clean around the corner.

OLD JOE: They would run out of that chicken once or twice a month.

STERLING: You could get a breast for fifty cents, a wing for a dime and a leg for a quarter. If you want you could get three chicken necks for a dime.

OLD JOE: They tore that down. June 28, 1974. Miss Harriet closed up her restaurant for the last time and walked straight from there to the hospital. They didn't know what was wrong with her. They ran some tests and found out she had a broken heart. She died three or four days after that.

STERLING: That was twenty years ago. They said they tore it down so they could build something. They ain't built nothing yet.

OLD JOE: They still tearing down. They trying to tear down my house.

STERLING: The house with the red door? You talking about Aunt Ester's house?

OLD JOE: I'm trying to stop them. That's like wrestling a bear.

STERLING: It ain't nothing to wrestle a bear if you know where to grab him. If you grab him by the balls you can get him to do anything you want.

OLD JOE: When was the last time you grabbed a bear by the balls? I prefer to have harmony.

HARMOND: We have harmony, Mr. Barlow. I'm not the enemy. But there are laws to make sure everything is done right.

OLD JOE: You trying to tear down my house is chaos. It ain't harmony. If we had harmony you'd be helping me paint it.

HARMOND: I've looked into the matter and I'm going to take care of it. We'll straighten it out. You have my word on that. But we have to follow the law.

(Old Joe acknowledges Harmond's lapel pin.)

OLD JOE: That's a nice pin you got there. That look like the flag.

HARMOND: Yeah that's the stars and stripes. I can get you one if you want one.

OLD JOE: Naw. I just say that's a nice pin. Nice colors. The Red White and Blue. We had a flag during the war. Company B, Fourth Battalion. Fellow named Joe Mott carried the flag. He got shot in the head on the second of November 1942. He was betting against it but he lost.

HARMOND: My brother died under that flag.

OLD JOE: Lots of men died under that flag. That American flag was everywhere. Joe Mott carried it into battle but it was everywhere. In the mess hall. In the dance hall. We had a great big mess hall and they would bring the women in from the town and we'd have a great big old dance. You look up and there would be that flag hanging behind the bandstand. That flag was everywhere. You saw it in the morning when you woke up and you saw it at night before you went to bed. Sometimes you saw it in your sleep. When the time come and I saw Joe Mott fall with that flag . . . shot right through the head . . . bullet went in one end and come out the other . . . I don't know where it went after that. When I saw him fall I said, "No, I ain't gonna let you get away with nothing like that." That's what I said when I picked up that flag. This the flag on *this* side of the battle. That's what side I'm on. Joe Mott ain't died for nothing. If his life don't mean nothing then my life don't mean nothing. I had sense enough to see that. A lot of people can't see that. I can't let him die and let the flag lay there. I was the closest one to it. I didn't even think about it. I just picked it up. I picked it up and carried it right up to the day I got discharged. December 4, 1945. I got out the Army and went and saw Joe Mott's mother. She live down in Georgia. I went down there and saw her. Walking down the street a white fellow stopped me. Reached up and tore my flag off my coat. Told me I ain't had no right to walk around with an American flag. I hope they let you keep yours.

(*Silence envelops the office.*)

HARMOND: When my brother got killed in Vietnam one of his buddies came to see my mother. At the funeral they gave her a flag. They folded it up real nice. She took it home and my father made her put it in a trunk. I never saw it again.

OLD JOE: It used to be I couldn't talk about your father. 'Cause I didn't have nothing nice to say about him. But now I can talk about him.

(Old Joe hands Harmond some papers.)

It says right there your father was the one who was paying taxes on the house.

HARMOND: My father was paying taxes on the house? Why?

OLD JOE: I don't know. His name is right there on the papers. Seem like you'd know more about that than me. Well if I was adding my two and two together it seem like to me you might want to find out.

(The lights go down on the scene.)

SCENE 5

The lights come up on Harmond in the office. Roosevelt enters, talking on his cell phone, laughing and having a good time.

ROOSEVELT: . . . I got to go now. *(Pause)* Naw, it ain't like that. *(Pause)* I told you I'm looking to eat my breakfast in a brand-new place. *(Pause)* Talk to you later.

(A big smile sets on Roosevelt as he hangs up. Harmond is looking at him.)

Arleen got me looking at other women.

HARMOND: You never stopped. How you gonna blame it on Arleen? You lucky she tolerate you.

ROOSEVELT: She do more than tolerate. I'm not talking about that. I'm talking about she got me when the field wasn't crowded. I don't know now. I don't know if she can go all the way with me.

HARMOND: She can't go all the way if you don't want her to. You got to figure that out. You can't wait to see if she's going to fit in. If you looking you looking . . . you can't blame it on her.

ROOSEVELT: I'm not blaming her. I just look around and see more out there than I did before. It's not her fault. She a good woman.

HARMOND: They hard to find. You better hold on to her.

ROOSEVELT: Hey Harmond, if the blight don't come through and we don't get the fed money, we can bring Bernie in as a partner. I already felt him out and know I can get him to go for it.

HARMOND: No shit he'd go for it. Bernie would love to get a piece of Bedford Hills. He'd have it so he'd be making money three ways. Owning part of the development, hiring his own construction firm and selling us all the supplies. Bedford Hills isn't going in Bernie Smith's pocket.

ROOSEVELT: Better than Bedford Hills sitting out there an empty lot. For all we know we're out here throwing money after nothing.

HARMOND: Sometimes you got to prime the pump. That's what gets the motor of big business going. The blight's good for everybody. It'll come through.

ROOSEVELT: I know how business goes. I figure WBTZ can be your campaign's official media sponsor. I'll give you a break on the ad rates.

HARMOND: I thought that was going to be your campaign contribution.

(Pulling out a file from the top of his desk) I need you to look over this. We got a problem with the house.

ROOSEVELT: What house?

HARMOND: 1839 Wylie.

ROOSEVELT: Man, we're working on a multimillion-dollar redevelopment project and you're still talking about some raggedy-ass, rodent-infested, unfit-for-human-habitation eyesore that they should have tore down twenty-five years ago.

HARMOND: We don't own the house.

ROOSEVELT: What you talking about? Bedford Hills paid you ten thousand dollars for that house. What do you mean we don't own it?

HARMOND: That was one of those houses Herm sent my way. I bought that house *before* it went to auction. Without the notice being published the sale was illegal.

ROOSEVELT: That's a technicality. I don't see where that makes a difference. The house was abandoned. The city claimed it for back taxes. You bought it from the city and then sold it to Bedford Hills. Case closed. What else is there?

HARMOND: Mr. Barlow has to be compensated.

ROOSEVELT: That old crazy motherfucker?

HARMOND: We're tearing down the man's house and he never received the proper notification that the city was selling it. We have to compensate him. That's the only thing I see to do.

ROOSEVELT: Okay . . . that's on you. You compensate him. You give him the ten grand you got from Bedford Hills if you want him to have it.

HARMOND: I also found out my father was paying the taxes on the house. I just can't figure out why.

ROOSEVELT: That don't surprise me. The people were probably paying their taxes through him. You know how that go. You get somebody that knows real estate to handle your business. I don't guess they were too sophisticated to know otherwise. I need somebody to help me with my real-estate taxes.

HARMOND: They couldn't have paid through him. Mr. Barlow said they never paid any taxes. The taxes were being paid *for* them.

ROOSEVELT: Okay, your father was paying the taxes. What difference does it make? The house is being torn down next month. We're having the groundbreaking. Everything's on track. Nothing but blue skies ahead.

HARMOND: So, Mr. Vice President of Mellon Bank, how are things going on your job?

ROOSEVELT: Man, I don't even want to go there. I get into work today and soon as I hit my office, John Albrecht's secretary's standing there in my doorway. She says John needs to see me in his office immediately. I felt like I was being called into the principal's office. So I get there and then the motherfucker makes me wait. When John can finally see me I go in and he tells me I'm not making my quotas. I'm not spending enough time at the office. Told me I don't have control of my team. Told me to conduct myself like a vice president. I started to tell him to kiss my ass but figured I'd wait a while. I'd wait until I had all my ducks lined up—

(The phone rings. Harmond answers it.)

HARMOND: Bedford Hills. *(Pause)* Yeah . . . Herm? What? *(Pause)* I can't hear you . . . huh? *(Pause)* When? *(Pause)* Hey Roosevelt, the city declared blight.

ROOSEVELT: Yes! Blight!

HARMOND *(Into the phone)*: Thanks, Herm. *(Hangs up)* Yeah, I told you the blight would come through.

ROOSEVELT: Blight! Blight! Blight! Blight!

(Roosevelt begins singing. Harmond eventually joins in.)

ROOSEVELT AND HARMOND:
Hail! Hail! The gang's all here,
It's one for all, the big and small,
It's always me for you.

No matter the weather
When we get together
It's always me for you . . .

(As they continue singing, Roosevelt begins to improvise:)

ROOSEVELT:
Blight! Blight! The gang's all here.
Blight! Blight! The gang's all here.
Blight! Blight! The gang's all here.

(Sterling enters as they are singing. He is bewildered by what he sees. They stop singing. Sterling walks over and throws a receipt on Harmond's desk.)

STERLING: Somebody owe me twenty-six dollars for my gallon of paint. And I want my money! I don't play, Harmond. I quit playing games when I was twelve.

HARMOND: What? What's the matter? What you talking about?

STERLING: I just painted that door and somebody come and put a X right over my paint job. I want my twenty-six dollars.

HARMOND: What door?

STERLING: You know what door I'm talking about. The red door. 1839 Wylie. Somebody put a X over my paint job.

(Harmond looks at Roosevelt.)

ROOSEVELT: That house is abandoned. We're going to tear it down. What you doing painting it? That don't make any sense. You're up there painting an abandoned house. Don't nobody owe you nothing.

(Harmond, understanding Sterling, goes into his pocket.)

HARMOND: Here. I'll give you twenty-six dollars but we're going to tear down the house. The matter is already settled.

STERLING: That ain't right.

HARMOND: Rightly or wrongly we're going to tear down the house.

STERLING: Wait a minute . . . wait a minute . . . say that again. Did I hear that shit right? "Rightly or wrongly" you're going to tear down Mr. Barlow's house. "Rightly or wrongly"? It don't matter to you if it's wrong?

HARMOND: I didn't say it didn't matter to me.

STERLING: It's got to matter. If it don't matter then nothing don't work. If nothing don't work then life ain't worth living. See, you living in a world where it don't matter. But that's not the world I live in. The world I live in right is right and right don't wrong nobody.

HARMOND: I'm talking reality. You have to face that reality whether you want to or not. Given the facts I don't understand why you would be up there painting the house in the first place.

STERLING: I'm painting the house 'cause Mr. Barlow hired me to paint it. You just can't tear down the man's house. That's the kind of shit they did to the Indians. They sign a treaty and soon as the Indians walk out the door they start plotting how to break it. I don't care what the law say. They liable to make a law that say anything. If they got a law say they can tear down his house they can make one say they can tear down yours. Common sense say that.

ROOSEVELT: I tell you what, my man. You go on and paint it. You paint it all you want to. Come next month we tearing the motherfucker down.

STERLING: If you fuck with Mr. Barlow's house . . . if you move one goddamn pebble . . . you gonna have to answer me on the battlefield. We can deal with this the old-fashioned way. It ain't gone out of style. It just got different levels. See . . .

(*He includes Harmond and Roosevelt in his announcement:*)

You the cowboys. I'm the Indians. See who win this war.

(*Sterling exits. The lights go down on the scene.*)

ACT TWO

SCENE 1

The lights come up on the office. In Harmond's area the campaign poster is up: "Hold Me to It—Harmond Wilks for Mayor." Harmond sits listening to the radio. Roosevelt's voice comes out of the radio.

ROOSEVELT: ". . . When you find yourself on the back nine and up by more than four strokes never forget you're always one stroke away from disaster. Take it one hole at a time. I learned this watching Neville Alcorn at the '88 Masters. He was a shot away from putting on the green jacket when he chose his seven iron from one hundred and eighty yards out. He could've made it in two strokes had he chosen his pitching wedge. With the seven iron you can get more distance but you give up ball control. The ball came out hot and looking for water. It took him ten strokes to finish the hole. That's why on the back nine you should always play it safe from the fairway. If you're up by

53

at least four strokes you can afford to be conservative. Also, to maintain ball control, remember to glide through your stroke. That's the best way to get to your putter. Next week I'll tell you the secret to getting your handicap down. This is 'Radio Golf' with Roosevelt Hicks. Making your game hotter with every stroke." (*Instrumental version of "Blue Skies" begins to play*) "Wishing you blue skies and stay out of the sand traps. WBTZ—It'll burn ya!"

(*Sterling enters with a flyer.*)

STERLING (*Reading the flyer*): "Come one, come all. Paint party, 1839 Wylie Avenue. Thursday, ten A.M. Music, dancing, refreshments." Put that up. I organized this. Let's see you tear down the house now. I know that house. That's Aunt Ester's house. You should go up there. I bet you ain't even been inside. Used to be a line to her door every Tuesday. I went up there to see Aunt Ester once. Had to go up to the red door three different times before she see me. She was sitting in this room. You had to go through some curtains into this room and she was just sitting there. Had this peacefulness about her. Aunt Ester told me I got good understanding. She say that before I could say anything to her. She just looked at me and said that. I talked to her a long while. Told her my whole life story. I asked her how old she was. She say she was three hundred and forty-nine years old. That was twenty-nine years ago. I was sorry to hear that she died. I went up to see Aunt Ester 'cause I was feeling sorry for myself for being an orphan and I was walking around carrying that. She told me set it down. "Make better what you have and you have best." Told me if I wanted to carry something carry some tools. I've been carrying tools ever since and I've been at peace with myself. You should go up there.

I got something else for you.

(Sterling exits and returns carrying Harmond's golf clubs.)

HARMOND: What you got there? Those are my golf clubs. Where'd you get my golf clubs!

STERLING: They used to be yours. They mine now. I paid twenty dollars for these golf clubs. *(Takes a club out of the bag)* What you supposed to do? You supposed to point your toes like this?

HARMOND: Where did you get my golf clubs from? They were stolen from my car. Those are mine! Where did you get them from?

STERLING: Give me twenty dollars and they yours.

HARMOND: Where did you get them from?

STERLING: I don't know what his name was. I know he was mad. He carrying them golf clubs around and couldn't find nobody to sell them to. I give him twenty dollars. That was more than anybody else would give him. He might have asked for thirty if he wasn't tired of carrying them. I'll let you have them for twenty dollars.

(Harmond gives him twenty dollars.)

HARMOND: I didn't know what I was going to do without these.

(Sterling discovers the campaign poster.)

STERLING: "Hold Me to It—Harmond Wilks for Mayor." You know how you can win the election hands down? You know how on the Parkway they have one lane they call a H-O-V lane and three lanes that ain't? All you got to do is switch it around and make them three lanes H-O-V lanes and the one lane for single drivers. That one lane be bumper to bumper and won't nobody wanna drive in it. After a while there won't be any single drivers. That one lane be empty all the time and the people be begging you to make it a H-O-V lane too. Then the whole thing be H-O-V. What you think?

HARMOND: You'd have a riot on your hands. The people wouldn't stand for that. You'd have mass civil disobedience. You couldn't get enough policemen to hand out tickets.

STERLING: Common sense say if you want to cut down on traffic you got to give the people an incentive. That's what the problem is now. People don't know how to think. You ever honk at anybody 'cause they wasn't going fast enough?

HARMOND: Yeah. I have honked at people.

STERLING: Where was they going?

HARMOND: Where were they going? I don't know where they were going.

STERLING: I know. I know where they was going. They was going to the next red light. You ever think of that? Everybody in a hurry to slow down. I think it's kinda funny if you think about it. You get to be mayor is you gonna be mayor of the black folks or the white folks?

HARMOND: If I win I'm going to be mayor of the City of Pittsburgh. I'm gonna be mayor of all the people.

STERLING: The white mayor he be the mayor of white folks. Black folks can't get the streets cleaned. The schools don't have no textbooks. Don't have no football uniforms. The mayor be the mayor for white folks. As soon as black folks start a club or something the first thing they say is it just ain't gonna be for blacks. Why not? They got five hundred thousand things that be just for white folks. If they have fourteen hundred students out at Pitt eating lunch in the cafeteria and they have five black people eating lunch together they say, "Look, see, they segregate themselves." They ain't said nothing about them thirteen hundred and ninety-five white folks eating lunch by themselves. What's wrong with being the mayor for black folks?

HARMOND: I'm going to be the mayor of everybody. It's not about being white or black, it's about being American. Did you see in the paper today where Cincinnati's trying to get Wilson Sporting Goods to relocate there? I'm working on a plan to bring them to Pittsburgh by putting together a hundred-million-dollar tax incentive based on manufacturing hours. Offer them that site for a manufacturing facility right there where the steel mill was. A hundred million dollars is a powerful incentive. Cincinnati's not going to do that. Plus you have the rivers and railroads. We have the airports and the banks. And this is a sports town. Cincinnati can't compete with us.

(Old Joe enters.)

STERLING: Hey Mr. Barlow, wait till you see that other side I painted. I changed the color to tone down the red a little bit. I mixed some white in there but not enough to make it pink. You're gonna like it. Did you figure out what color green you wanted?

OLD JOE: Every time I hear the word "green" I think of Sam Green. Did you know Sam Green? You can't be nobody but who you are. That's when I first found that out. Sam Green was a black man used to own a grocery store down on Fullerton Street. Green's Groceries. That was the biggest grocery store down there. Used to sell live chickens and have the vegetables sitting out on the sidewalk. Everybody used to shop at Green's Groceries. He went out to Shadyside to buy some furniture and the police arrested him. Say he looked suspicious. He can't look no other way than the way he look. He found out he living with people who look at him with suspicion. Wherever he go and whatever he do. He found that out and that sent him straight to the hospital. Had to haul him away in a straitjacket. They took him over to Mayview. He still there, I believe. If he ain't died. He might be dead 'cause living like that is hard on your body.

HARMOND: Mr. Barlow, it's good to see you. I have something for you.

OLD JOE: It ain't no bread pudding, is it? I was just thinking about some bread pudding. You like bread pudding? My mother used to make bread pudding. She made the best bread pudding. She didn't do it too often but when she did she used to make a great big old pan last two or three days. It ain't no bread pudding, is it?

(Harmond hands Old Joe a check for ten thousand dollars. Old Joe looks at it and hands it back to him.)

This got my name on it but it don't belong to me. Here, you take it.

HARMOND: No, that's for your house. I looked into it and the city didn't notify you that they were putting it up for sale. That's compensation for your house.

OLD JOE: That's too much money. I wouldn't know what to do with that much money. Go on, you take it. I don't want it. I got enough troubles as it is.

HARMOND: This isn't any trouble. This is what Bedford Hills is paying you for your house. The city sold your house because you owed over twelve thousand dollars back taxes. This is what they sold it for.

OLD JOE: I like my house. Don't you like your house?

HARMOND: It's not a matter of if I like my house or not. Or if you like your house. Come Thursday your house is going to be torn down to make way for a redevelopment project. We're going to put a ten-story apartment building on that site with a hundred and eighty apartments. It's not a matter of if you like your house.

OLD JOE: I remember you had a porch. A white porch and sometimes you would sit up there out the rain. We didn't have no porch. If we wasn't careful we could drown. You had chairs. We'd sit on the stoop. But we all sitting just the same. If you ask somebody what they was doing they'd tell you they was sitting. We'd sit there and that was the best expression of life. At that time. Another time it be something else. You always looking to express yourself. Not in one or two things . . . but in everything. Even the way you scratch your head. The way you walk across the yard. The way you sit. All that's like talking. We'd sit out there in the yard. You didn't have to say anything. You didn't have to have no other meaning. Everybody just sitting out. That was some of the best times I had in life. I like my house. I was thinking about getting a new roof.

HARMOND: That house is being torn down! I don't know why you can't understand that. You have to take this check. Even if the city hadn't sold the house you'd still have to pay the back taxes.

OLD JOE: That's what I told myself . . . the taxes come first. Only thing I don't know if I'm gonna live long enough to pay them off. I can't pay but a hundred dollars a month. So maybe I better get a new roof first so it don't rain on me while I pay the taxes.

(Old Joe exits.)

HARMOND: The house is being torn down on Thursday. Can't he see that? I'm trying to help him. This way at least he has something. If he doesn't take the ten thousand dollars he won't have anything. It doesn't make any sense. Can't you talk to him and get him to see that?

STERLING: See now Harmond, I thought you was a smart man. When you gave me that twenty dollars you bought some stolen property. You can go to jail for that. You know how many niggers in jail for receiving stolen goods? Harmond Wilks, candidate for mayor, arrested for receiving stolen goods.

59

HARMOND: Those are my golf clubs! Got my initials on the bag. Look at that. H. W. These are mine!

STERLING: That's Mr. Barlow's house. Go up there. Got his initials on it. 1839 Wylie. Only he was smarter than you. He ain't broke no laws. You stole Mr. Barlow's house. As it is Bedford Hills is in possession of stolen property and you and him are the only ones who know you stole it. Everybody else thinks you bought it. That's why he can't call the police. Won't nobody listen to him. He trying to get them to listen. He shouting and nobody paying attention. If you even *whisper* everybody sit up and stop to listen.

(Sterling gives Harmond back the twenty dollars.)

Here, I don't want your twenty dollars. Take the golf clubs as a present.

HARMOND: That's not the same thing.

STERLING: It look like the same thing to me. But then maybe I'm wrong. What do I know? I ain't went to school to study up on it. But some things you don't have to study up on. You ain't got to study up on right and wrong.

(Sterling exits. The lights go down on the scene.)

SCENE 2

The lights come up on Roosevelt practicing his golf swing in the office. Roosevelt's area is cluttered with WBTZ paraphernalia: bumper stickers, posters, a calendar, etc. Harmond enters carrying a wrapped parcel. Roosevelt pulls a new set of keys out of his pocket.

ROOSEVELT: Hey Harmond, look at these. Picked them up at the station today.

(Roosevelt tosses the keys to Harmond.)

Those keys will open every door of 255 Penn Avenue. I can go wherever I want. I picked up those keys and then walked straight over to the bank. Went right past John Albrecht's secretary. She didn't know what to do. She never seen nobody walk right in John Albrecht's office before. Neither did he. I walked right in, before he could say anything I told him, "Kiss my ass. I quit." His face turned pink as his shirt. So he don't forget me I'm gonna send the motherfucker a Christmas card every year.

HARMOND: Congratulations. You know how many people would love to do that?

ROOSEVELT: My new office is getting painted today. Light money green. Wait till you see the view. When the new stadium's built, I'll be able to *almost* watch the Pirates play. And my new business cards are on rush order. I'm giving you the first one.

HARMOND: I'm real happy for you. I hope this leads you to where you're going.

ROOSEVELT: Now that you got your clubs back let's go play a round to celebrate. This one's on you.

HARMOND: I can't. I got a lot to do. I went up and looked at that house on Wylie. Have you ever been inside?

ROOSEVELT: Naw, I haven't been inside it. I ain't that brave. I'd be afraid it would collapse on me.

HARMOND: It's a Federalist brick house with a good double-base foundation. I couldn't believe it. It has beveled glass on every floor. There's a huge stained-glass window leading up to the landing. And the staircase is made of Brazilian wood with a hand-carved balustrade. You don't see that too often.

ROOSEVELT: That's 'cause people don't like that kind of shit anymore. All that's listed in the demolition contract. They have salvage rights. That's why we got a good price on the demolition.

HARMOND: You should feel the woodwork. If you run your hand slow over some of the wood you can make out these carvings. There's faces. Lines making letters. An old language. And there's this smell in the air.

ROOSEVELT: That's them mothballs. People used to throw mothballs all through their old shit. They'll stink up the air like that.

HARMOND: No . . . The air in the house smells sweet like a new day.

(Gets the parcel) You need to look over this. There are adjustments that need to be made to the development plan. We have to anticipate what the fallout will be.

ROOSEVELT: What adjustments? What are you talking about?

HARMOND: I'll take care of it. I'll take the heat. I'm going to start making the calls today. But you need to be aware of this. I got a jumpstart and had a new rendering made.

(Harmond unwraps the parcel. It is a new rendering that features a photograph of 1839 Wylie preserved with the complex built around it.)

ROOSEVELT: What the fuck is that?

HARMOND: It's a relatively easy adjustment. See . . . We pull back the south wing . . . All we lose in the long run are thirty-two parking spaces.

ROOSEVELT: What the fuck is that ugly-ass house sitting there for?

HARMOND: Mr. Barlow wouldn't accept the payment for his house.

ROOSEVELT: So what? He didn't take the money proves he's crazy. Put the ten thousand back in your pocket where it belongs.

HARMOND: He won't accept compensation because his house isn't for sale. We have no choice but to build around it. We don't own the house.

ROOSEVELT: Harmond, where you at, man? That's a dead issue. I don't care now if the pope owned it. Come Thursday that house is history. (*Pulls out the original rendering*) Look at this. All the money's lined up. We got contracts with Whole Foods and with Starbucks and Barnes & Noble. All finalized. It's all set and agreed to. We can't fuck with it now. I worked hard to get this. We have to stick to the plan. I got a lot invested in this.

HARMOND: I have a lot invested in it too. We can still do the plan. We're just altering it. We can't tear down a house we don't own. It's the law.

ROOSEVELT: The house is being torn down Thursday, ten A.M. whether we own it or not. It's still being torn down. I'm going down the club and take a sauna. Then I got to go over to the station. We can talk about this house shit later. Don't move forward on any of this without me.

(*Roosevelt exits. Harmond goes over and stares at the rendering. He goes to his desk and picks up the phone and dials.*)

HARMOND: Hey Hop, Harmond here. You know that house on Wylie? We're not going to tear that down. (*Pause*) Yeah, I know. We'll pay the fee. (*Pause*) Naw, it's not you. You do good work. I'll call you on the next one. (*Pause*) All right. Thanks, Hop. (*Hangs up*)

(*Old Joe enters.*)

OLD JOE: Here. (*Hands Harmond a hundred dollars*) I got a hundred dollars. That's the most I can pay for my taxes at one time. Who do I pay? Do I pay you? I don't want to get behind. I got behind in my life insurance but I caught up. I don't want to be a burden on nobody. White folks don't be a burden on their kids. If you white and your daddy die you get some money. If you black you get a bill from the undertaker.

HARMOND: We're not going to tear down the house.

(Old Joe takes back the hundred dollars.)

OLD JOE: They say if you live long enough the boat will turn around. Big boats turn slow but they turn nonetheless.

(Harmond shows the rendering to Old Joe.)

HARMOND: Take a look at this. See . . . There's your house and we're going to build our development around it.

OLD JOE: Where the yard at? The house got a yard. Where my daughter gonna plant her garden?

HARMOND: We'll have the surveyors come out to make sure all the original property stays intact.

OLD JOE: Where my deed at? Just 'cause you say that don't mean it's true.

HARMOND: We'll transfer the deed and get it recorded. But remember you have to keep up with the taxes now.

(Old Joe starts to leave.)

OLD JOE: I can tell my daughter to start packing.

HARMOND: Mr. Barlow, I looked into why my father was paying taxes on the house. He was doing what my grandfather started. But I can't figure out why. Have you ever heard of Caesar Wilks?

OLD JOE: I never heard that name.

HARMOND: Did you ever hear your family mention anybody with the Wilks name?

OLD JOE: No. Nobody talked about the Wilks. I never heard nobody say that name in the family.

HARMOND: Not many speak well of my father. He was a hard businessman. You shook his hand on a deal knowing he always got the better end of it. But he was an honest man. My father talked a lot about family. He said that family was the most important thing. Yet when my brother got killed in Vietnam he didn't go to his funeral. He planned for Raymond and me to go to Cornell, then take over Wilks Realty. But Raymond didn't follow the plan. He wanted to go to Grambling and play football. My father said he wouldn't pay for it. Raymond joined the Army to pay for it himself. I followed the plan and went to Cornell. They sent Raymond to Vietnam and he got killed. My father turned blood into vinegar. He didn't even go to Raymond's funeral. I could never look at my father the same after that. Even though he betrayed those values I still clung to them. But what I can't figure out is why my family was paying the taxes on your house.

OLD JOE: Maybe they used to own the house.

HARMOND: No. We never owned 1839 Wylie.

OLD JOE: I remember about the time Black Mary was born there was a lot of talk about the house.

HARMOND: Black Mary?

OLD JOE: That's my daughter. I named her after my mother. Lots of people do that. Old folks used to do that all the time.

HARMOND: I thought your mother's name was Ester Tyler.

OLD JOE: It was. But that wasn't her birth name. She didn't tell nobody what that was. Now that she's dead I guess it don't matter. When you dead you done. Her birth name was Black Mary.

HARMOND: My grandfather had a sister named Black Mary. I thought she died before I was born.

OLD JOE: Lots of people named Black Mary. That's a nice name.

HARMOND: My grandfather was named Caesar Wilks and he had a sister named Black Mary. They had different mothers but they had the same father. I know the name of their father. Do you know the name of your grandfather?

OLD JOE: Yeah. But I ain't gonna tell you. But I'll write it down. You write it down too.

(*They each write the name on a piece of paper. They recognize that this is one of the important moments of their lives in which everything may change for them. Old Joe hands his paper to Harmond. Harmond looks at the paper. Old Joe waits to find out the truth.*)

HARMOND (*Smiling broadly as he reads*): Henry Samuels.

(*Harmond wraps Old Joe in his arms. The lights go down on the scene.*)

SCENE 3

The lights come up on Mame and Roosevelt in the office.

ROOSEVELT: What did you tell him?

MAME: I told him we wanted to talk with him. He said he was on the way.

ROOSEVELT: I never seen him this way before. He's been talking a lot about his father and his brother. He's got to let that go.

MAME: All Harmond talked about last night was that old man being some cousin of his. He stayed up all night. I don't know what time he came to bed.

ROOSEVELT: He's lost sight of what's important. I'm worried. He's working too hard.

MAME: He wants to move to the Hill. Wants to move back in the house he grew up in. Harmond hasn't lived in the Hill in twenty-five years. I can't move back here, Roosevelt.

I don't want to go backward. I wasn't born backward. You'd be surprised how many white people think all black people live in the Hill.

(Harmond enters.)

HARMOND: You been waiting long? I would've been here earlier but I got a call back from Starbucks in Seattle. They still need to see the new drawings but they love the idea. They think it will make great publicity about preserving the house, preserving part of the community. At the Grand Opening they're going to give Mr. Barlow free Starbucks coffee for life.

MAME: Harmond . . . Slow down. We want to talk with you. You're working too hard. I think we should go away for the weekend. You've always talked about going to San Francisco. This would be a good time to go. Not too many tourists. The hotels will be half empty.

HARMOND: What about the groundbreaking? I can't go away till after the campaign. Then we can go to San Francisco. Whether it's a good time to go or not.

ROOSEVELT: Herman's got a place in the Caribbean. You can go down there for a few days. Play some golf. Go sailing. Just get your mind off everything. I can deal with things till you get back.

MAME: We can postpone the groundbreaking. Things will smooth over. When you come back you'll be fresh.

HARMOND: Why? Everything's coming together. I'm staying on top of everything. Plans change and you got to roll with them. Bedford Hills is on schedule. Everything's still set for the groundbreaking next week. There's no reason to change that.

ROOSEVELT: Harmond, man, you need to step back. Get some perspective. I've been putting out fires all day, cleaning up after you. You made a mess. At ten o'clock this morning, there was no Bedford Hills. The project collapsed. I've been dancing on the phone for hours trying to bring it back.

HARMOND: What are you talking about?

ROOSEVELT: Whole Foods was so pissed it took me an hour to get somebody to take my call. They were ready to pull out. So was Barnes & Noble. We signed a contract. We can't change their store layout and cut their customer parking in half. Then I get a call from the committee chair who gave us the fed money. He wanted to *remind* me that the use of that grant money was contingent on us following the plan submitted in our proposal. And don't forget we got a hundred and eighty apartment units to rent. Leaving that piece-of-shit house standing there we might as well turn them apartments right now over to the projects. Harmond, you're off the hook with this. There's no way you can save that house.

HARMOND: Everybody involved in this project wants to see it happen. They'll get mad at first but they'll calm down and adjust. The plan I came up with is the only way I see we can move forward. We can't tear down Mr. Barlow's house.

ROOSEVELT: Mr. Barlow? Let me tell you about that old crazy motherfucker. (*Rummages about his desk until he finds a set of papers*) Here's your Mr. Barlow. I had Sergeant Griffin fax me this.

(*Roosevelt scans and reads from the rap sheet excerpts that strike his eye:*)

Fraud. Hijacking. Grand theft. Assault. Loitering. Drunkenness. Disturbing the peace. Vagrancy. He has a record go all the way back to 1937. Stole a crate of chickens in 1938. Burglary. First-degree assault. Born 1918. Highest grade completed: fourth. Married. Divorced. Married. Divorced. Defendant says he is the father of eight children, ages six to eighteen. This was in 1942. Probably didn't take care of any of them. He too busy stealing. Spent eight months on the county farm, 1939. Discharged from Army in 1945. Two years for assault of a police officer, 1948. Three years Western State Penitentiary for hijacking, 1952. Thirty days loitering, 1957. Sixty days vagrancy, 1958. Spent four months in Mayview State Hospital. Sent for ninety-day observation. Was kept an additional thirty days for further observation. It wouldn't have taken me but thirty minutes to tell he's not all there. Defendant reports his address as 1839 Wylie. Was caught breaking and entering. Defendant claims to have lost key to said residence. Here you go! This what I'm talking about. This is how crazy that nigger is. Defendant claims to be a member of a lost tribe said to have migrated from the Arabian peninsula five hundred B.C. Defendant states he wants to bring charges against the United States Government for harboring kidnappers. Claims to have journeyed to a City of Bones sunken in the Atlantic Ocean. See? I told you. You can't get any crazier than that.

HARMOND: All that doesn't matter. That doesn't mean anything. I don't care if he is a criminal. We can't tear down his house. I've got a plan for Bedford Hills that will still work. But we need to start working together on this. We can get everybody back on board. I'll call Whole Foods tomorrow.

(There is an awkward silence.)

ROOSEVELT: Harmond, you're not listening, man. I called up and had the demolition of 1839 Wylie rescheduled for Thursday so everything can go according to the original plan.

HARMOND: How can you do that? You're the one not listening. We're not going to tear down a house we don't own.

ROOSEVELT: You don't own it. You're getting this confused with Wilks Realty. This is Bedford Hills Redevelopment. That's who owns 1839 Wylie and I called up and got the demolition rescheduled. You're not the only one calling the shots.

HARMOND (*Taking this all in*): Okay. Okay. Bedford Hills owns 1839 Wylie. Okay. But Bedford Hills acquired 1839 Wylie illegally. It bought it from me but I didn't own it. I bought the house before it went to auction. That's against the law. That's corruption. I'm going down to the courthouse and file an injunction to stop the demolition.

MAME: Harmond, if you do that you're throwing everything away. All our hard work. Your career. Your reputation . . .

HARMOND: You got to have rule of law. Otherwise it would be chaos. Nobody wants to live in chaos.

(*Harmond exits. The lights go down on the scene.*)

SCENE 4

The lights come up on Harmond on his cell phone. The office phone is ringing. Harmond ignores it.

HARMOND: No, I won't do any interviews. (*Pause*) Tell them I'll have a statement for them later. I don't have any comment at this time. (*Pause*) I don't care who it is. (*Pause*)

(*The phone stops ringing.*)

Keep trying to get a hold of Herman. Have him call me on my cell. Okay.

(*He hangs up. The office phone rings again. Harmond ignores it. He makes a call on his cell phone.*)

Hey, Roosevelt. Harmond here. Letting you know I'm at the office.

(He hangs up. The office phone continues ringing. Harmond is pulling the phone cords out of the wall when Mame enters. Harmond stops to look at her. She doesn't say anything.)

We need to put together a statement for the press. If I don't respond it looks like I did something wrong.

MAME: When do they rule on the injunction?

HARMOND: Today. Tomorrow. Next week. A month from now. Whenever the judge feels like it. But he has to take the case first. I've drawn up an affidavit Herman needs to sign. Till I can get on the docket, I was granted a temporary injunction to stop the demolition.

MAME: I just drove by the site. They got two bulldozers sitting up there.

HARMOND: What are you talking about bulldozers? They can't tear down the house. I got a temporary injunction.

MAME: There's a bunch of people up there too. They're passing out these flyers. *(Reads from the flyer)* "Come one, come all. Paint party, 1839 Wylie Avenue. Thursday, ten A.M." That's just what they're having . . . a party. Got music blasting. Got the barbecue cooking. Kids running around. Looks like the Fourth of July.

HARMOND: I don't care what's going on. They can't tear down the house today.

MAME *(Looking at the campaign poster)*: "Hold Me to It— Harmond Wilks for Mayor." Mayor Wilks . . . That was almost you. You could've been mayor, then governor, then Senator Wilks. All that was ahead for you. It was right there. All you had to do was follow the plan.

HARMOND: I've been following plans my whole goddamn life. My father set Wilks Realty out before me when I got out of school. All I had to do was follow the plan. It was a

Monday. I got up that morning and went into work with him. We walked in Wilks Realty and there on one of the doors was my name: "Harmond Wilks." That looked good. I thought, "Yeah, this is what I'm supposed to do." My father didn't say anything to me about it. He walked ahead into his office and I walked into mine. Sat there at the desk. Now what? There were new tablets . . . new pens in the drawers. I sat there a while. Then the phone rang and I answered it. All I had to do was follow the plan. I can't follow the plan this time, Mame. I'm afraid you look away from what's right too long you won't turn back. Start all the time looking for what's in this for me.

MAME: I got a call this morning from the governor's office. They canceled my next interview and said they didn't want to reschedule any further interviews with me at this time.

HARMOND: I'm sorry, Mame. I don't know what to say . . .

MAME: You jumped but I'm falling too. I'm the wife of Harmond Wilks. That's all the governor sees. All any of the other board members see. What all our friends see. I tied myself so tight to you that there is no me. I don't know if I can carry this any further.

HARMOND: Wait a minute. Wait a minute. What are you saying? You have been part of me for so long I wouldn't know what to do. What is life? Why am I living it? I've been trying to answer those questions. You are part of the answer. There are other answers but I wouldn't know how to go about finding them without you. You have to have a center. Without that center everything caves in.

MAME: I have a center too. What happens when that caves in? I have questions too. You're acting like a kid who because things don't go his way takes his ball and goes home. That's what your problem is. You've always been the kid who had the ball. You're the one with the glove and the bat. You had the bike when nobody else had one. All your life you always had everything go your way.

HARMOND: Everything went my father's way. Asking myself every day what would he do. Now I've got to follow my own plan like my brother did. But I need you beside me. You remember that time when we had just started dating? We were going to some big event you had planned. It was raining. I remember that event was a big night for you.

MAME: That was a big night. All eyes in the office were on me.

HARMOND: And I blew a tire on the way. There you were all dressed up. You didn't sit in the car. You were standing out along the road beside me. That red scarf wrapped pretty around your neck. You didn't get mad. You didn't blame me. We worked through it together. I still remember you standing out there holding out your hands ready to take the rusty bolts. That's when I knew that I loved you.

MAME: I'm still standing here, Harmond. I still love you. But this is all you now. Your campaign, that old house, the Hill . . . You're on your own with all that. I can't live my life for you. And you can't live yours for me. But I'm still standing here.

(Harmond takes Mame up in his arms for a long embrace. His cell phone begins to ring.)

See you tonight.

(Mame exits. Harmond answers the phone.)

HARMOND: Herm . . . *(Pause)* Listen, Herm. Listen . . . *(Pause)* Naw, they can't do that. They're just trying to scare you. *(Pause)* They can't nail you for anything. *(Pause)* Just sign the affidavit. I need it to make the case. *(Pause)* There's no way they can charge you with criminal intent. All the affidavit states is that the city sold me the block of houses off auction as a measure of expediency. And we have proof they were all purchased at market rate. You're clean on this. *(Pause)* Herm, trust me. *(Pause)* I can't do that. *(Pause)* I can't. I have to move forward with this. *(Pause)* Herm . . . Herm?

(The line is dead; Harmond hangs up. He looks over the office. Things have changed. He goes to his campaign poster and takes it down. He looks at it a while, then shakes his head and smiles. He tears the poster in half and throws it away. Sterling enters with a newspaper, a can of paint and a paintbrush.)

STERLING: Harmond Wilks . . . a desperado. *(Reads from the newspaper)* "Prominent Hill District Realtor Harmond Wilks yesterday alleged that the city has been selling property seized for real-estate taxes without holding a sheriff's auction. Wilks claims to have first-hand knowledge, having been involved in such backroom dealings over the years. The district attorney's office has yet to announce an investigation into Wilks's allegations. Rumored to be the Democrats' choice for mayor, this may put Wilks's potential candidacy in jeopardy." That's kinda funny. You usually be the sheriff or the captain or something like that. Now you a desperado.

HARMOND: We're not tearing down the house.

STERLING: The sign says "Demolition. Thursday, ten A.M."

HARMOND: They can't tear down the house today. I was granted a temporary injunction to stop the demolition.

STERLING: But you still gonna need a lawyer. You can go down to Hill House. They got some lawyers down there. See if you can get a white lawyer. White crimes, white lawyer, country-club jail. Black crimes, black lawyer, Western State Penitentiary.

HARMOND: I'm my own lawyer. I got the law on my side.

STERLING: You got too big too fast. They don't like that. If you hadn't did it to yourself they was laying for you. They don't mind you playing their game but you can't outplay them. If you score too many points they change the rules. That's what the problem was . . . you scored too many points. If things had kept on going like that you was gonna have to buy you a gun. Time this is over you ain't gonna be able to walk down the street without somebody pointing at you. If they point *and* whisper you in trouble. You'd have to move out the state. Start over again somewhere fresh. That is if you still wanna play the game. If you still wanna play the game you gonna have to relearn the rules. See . . . they done changed. If you relearn the rules they'll let you back on the playing field. But now you crippled. You ain't got but one leg. You be driving around looking for handicapped parking. Get back on the field and every time you walk by somebody they check their pockets. That's enough to kill anybody right there. If you had to take a little hit like that all day every day how long you think you can last? I give you six months.

HARMOND: I know how the game is played. I know the rules.

STERLING: But do you know when the game is over. When you in an argument the best thing to do is to stop arguing. I got in an argument with Buddy Will over Muhammad Ali. Buddy said Muhammad Ali won all his fights by outthinking everybody. Say he used psychology. I asked him what the hell his hands were doing while his mind was thinking. Told him to go ask Joe Frazier what they were doing. He ain't had enough sense to see what I was saying, so I say, "You right." And walked away. That's what you got to do. Like that man stole three hundred million dollars. He say, "You right." They fined him thirty million dollars and give him a year in jail. The way I figure that leave him two hundred and seventy million dollars profit. Unless my math is wrong. Giving in is good for your blood pressure too. Your heart and everything else.

(Roosevelt enters.)

ROOSEVELT (*To Sterling*): Look, my man. This ain't no hang-out spot. Go hang out on the corner.

STERLING: I'm talking to Mr. Wilks.

ROOSEVELT: Mr. Wilks is busy right now. We're having a meeting. You got to go somewhere else.

STERLING: What? You think I'm a stray dog? I'm homeless? I ain't got no friends? I ain't got no purpose in life? You the big man. You got everything. You got more reason to live than I do. What you got I ain't got? I got good manners and everything. What you got? What makes you special? I got a house. I got everything you got. Plus a little bit more. I got common sense. I know riddles. I can sing. And I used to have a pretty good hoop game. What you got I ain't got? I got a dick. I got a fist. I got a gun. I got a knife. What you got?

ROOSEVELT: For one, I got some money.

STERLING: I got money too. You think you the only one got money. Money make you special?

(*Sterling goes into his pocket and takes out some bills.*)

There. Now what? Show me your money. Come on. Show me your money. I ain't sure you got none. There's mine. Where's yours?

ROOSEVELT: I said money. You don't know what money is. When I go to the bank I need a wheelbarrow. They send me straight to the weighing station. Say they weigh it up now and count it later.

STERLING: You know what you are? It took me a while to figure it out. You a Negro. White people will get confused and call you a nigger but they don't know like I know. I know the truth of it. I'm a nigger. Negroes are the worst thing in God's creation. Niggers got style. Negroes got blindyitis. A dog knows it's a dog. A cat knows it's a cat. But a Negro don't know he's a Negro. He thinks he's a white man. It's Negroes like you who hold us back.

ROOSEVELT: Who's "us"? Roosevelt Hicks is not part of any "us." It's not my fault if your daddy's in jail, your mama's on drugs, your little sister's pregnant and the kids don't have any food 'cause the welfare cut off the money. Roosevelt Hicks ain't holding nobody back. Roosevelt Hicks got money. Roosevelt Hicks got a job because Roosevelt Hicks wanted one. You niggers kill me blaming somebody else for your troubles. Get up off your ass . . . quit stealing . . . quit using drugs . . . go to school . . . get a job . . . pay your taxes. Oh, I see, you can't do that 'cause Roosevelt Hicks is holding you back.

STERLING: Yeah, you holding me back. You make things hard for me. You go around kissing the white man's ass then when they see me they think I'm supposed to kiss it too. You ever notice how glad they are when they see you coming. Go on downtown and kiss some more ass 'cause you ain't wanted around here. I'm talking to Mr. Wilks.

ROOSEVELT: You're loitering. You're disrupting a place of business. If you don't leave I'm calling the police.

(Sterling goes over to the paint can and opens it. He dips his finger in, then makes a line from his forehead down to his nose.)

STERLING: Look at that. You know what that is? That's a mark. I'm marking myself 'cause I don't want you to misunderstand this.

(He dips his hand in the paint and marks both sides of his cheeks.)

See that?

(He marks his face again.)

I learned that from Cochise. We on the battlefield now.

(Sterling exits.)

ROOSEVELT: Each one crazier than the next. I always told myself niggers could be doing a little better than they was doing. I thought it was because they was lazy but I see now these niggers done let the white man drive them crazy. Now you take this man. He didn't grow up. He still playing cowboys and Indians. He hasn't stopped to think about how he's going to get that paint off of his face. Now why he do that? Why is he walking around with a can of paint? We haven't got to that part yet. That's the part which proves the equation. Here's a man who's painting a house that is going to be torn down. Now you think about that a minute. They are going to tear down the house and he declares war on me. He doesn't have enough sense to know who the enemy is. I'm not the enemy. The enemy is right in his mirror. I don't understand. There isn't much I understand anymore. I don't understand you. I stood by and watched you commit suicide. For what? A raggedy-ass house. I don't understand. And you don't have nothing to show for it. The judge threw out the injunction. He ordered the demolition. The bulldozers are up there now.

HARMOND: I was granted a temporary injunction. That's the law.

ROOSEVELT: The judge dismissed the temporary injunction and ordered the demolition.

HARMOND: They can't do that! What about the law?

ROOSEVELT: Bulldozers start at 10:15.

HARMOND: This is chaos! Right and wrong don't matter.

ROOSEVELT: Harmond, did you really think the judge was going to let that raggedy-ass house stand in the way of a multi-million-dollar redevelopment project that's spearheaded by the city? Common sense would tell you otherwise.

HARMOND: No. Common sense says that ain't right. We see it different. No matter what you always on the edge. If you go to the center you look up and find everything done shifted and the center is now the edge. The rules change every day. You got to change with them. After a while the edge starts to get worn. You don't notice it at first but you're fraying with it. Oh, no, look . . . We got a black mayor. We got a black CEO. The head of our department is black. We couldn't possibly be prejudiced. Got two hundred and fourteen people work in the department and two blacks but we couldn't possibly be race-conscious. Look, we even got a black football coach. You guys can sing. You can run fast. Boy, I love Nat King Cole. I love Michael Jordan. I just love him. We got a black guy works in management. Twenty-four million blacks living in poverty but it's their fault. Look, we got a black astronaut. I just love Oprah. How do you guys dance like that? After a while that center starts to give. They keep making up the rules as you go along. They keep changing the maps. Then you realize you're never going to get to that center. It's all a house of cards. Everything resting on a slim edge. Looking back you can see it all. Wasn't nothing solid about it. Everything was an *if* and a *when* and a *maybe*. Of course . . . but not really. Yes . . . but not really. I don't want to live my life like that, Roosevelt.

ROOSEVELT: Yeah. I understand. But Harmond. Look. I don't know how to say this . . . I'm buying you out.

HARMOND: Buying me out? You're buying me out?

ROOSEVELT: It's in the charter.

HARMOND: How are you gonna buy me out? You can't buy me out of my own company.

ROOSEVELT: I can force a buyout. If one of the partners jeopardizes the business by straying from the company's initial charter the other partner can force the sale to protect the company's financing structure. We don't have to go public with this.

HARMOND: How are you gonna buy me out? Where are you gonna come up with that kind of money?

(Harmond stops and looks at Roosevelt.)

Oh, I see! Bernie Smith . . . Bernie's calling in his chips. He used you for the radio station. Now he's using you to get half a stake in a prime redevelopment site that's being funded by the federal government. But he still needs minority involvement. He still needs a black face on the enterprise. Like he needed minority involvement to buy the radio station. Enter Roosevelt Hicks. The shuffling, grinning nigger in the woodpile. How much he pay for something like that? After he rolls over and puts his pants back on, what you got? A hundred dollars? Three hundred dollars? Or are you one of them high-class thousand-dollar whores?

ROOSEVELT: Whoa! Wait a minute. I'm not going to be anybody's whore. Just because shit didn't go your way you just can't go and call me out my name. My name is Roosevelt Hicks. I am part owner of WBTZ radio and I am not anybody's whore. Let's get that straight. I'm buying you out 'cause you jeopardized our project when you started all this shit about that goddamn house. You can't blame me for that.

HARMOND: Yeah. Yeah. I see. I see now. Got you! I see who you are. Yeah! Yeah! Buy me out!

ROOSEVELT: You're wrong, Harmond. You can believe what you want to believe. It didn't go down like that. You're the one who fucked-up everything.

HARMOND: Bedford Hills may own 1839 Wylie. And they may be tearing it down today. But Wilks Realty owns this office.

(Roosevelt looks at Harmond and gets his meaning.)

ROOSEVELT: Okay, man. You got that.

(*Roosevelt gathers up some things from his desk and puts them in a box and starts for the door. Harmond takes down the Tiger Woods poster from the wall.*)

HARMOND: Here. Take this with you.

ROOSEVELT: I'm disappointed in you, Harmond. But hey, that's part of life too. I'll see you around, man.

(*Roosevelt steps toward the door, his arms full. Harmond helps him by opening the door for him. A genuine and painful good-bye.*)

HARMOND: Don't take no wooden nickels.

(*Roosevelt exits. Harmond closes the door. He turns around and discovers the office is empty. He takes the WBTZ poster, looks at it for a moment, then drops it in the trash. He discovers the paintbrush left on the desk. He takes off his coat and rolls up his sleeves. He picks up the paintbrush and exits. "Hail, Hail, the Gang's All Here" is heard as the lights go down on the scene.*)

BLACK

[*Broadway production note: Harmond painted warrior markings on his face, similar to Sterling's actions, then exited the office, paintbrush in hand.*]

August Wilson

April 27, 1945–October 2, 2005

August Wilson authored *Gem of the Ocean, Joe Turner's Come and Gone, Ma Rainey's Black Bottom, The Piano Lesson, Seven Guitars, Fences, Two Trains Running, Jitney, King Hedley II* and *Radio Golf*. These works explore the heritage and experience of African Americans, decade by decade, over the course of the twentieth century. Mr. Wilson's plays have been produced at regional theaters across the country, on Broadway and throughout the world. In 2003, Mr. Wilson made his professional stage debut in his one-man show *How I Learned What I Learned*.

Mr. Wilson's work garnered many awards, including the Pulitzer Prize for *Fences* (1987) and *The Piano Lesson* (1990); a Tony Award for *Fences*; Great Britain's Olivier Award for *Jitney*; and eight New York Drama Critics Circle awards for *Ma Rainey's Black Bottom, Fences, Joe Turner's Come and Gone, The Piano Lesson, Two Trains Running, Seven Guitars, Jitney* and *Radio Golf*. Additionally, the cast recording of *Ma Rainey's Black Bottom* received a 1985 Grammy Award, and Mr. Wilson received a 1995 Emmy Award nomination for his screenplay adaptation of *The Piano Lesson*. Mr. Wilson's early works include the one-act plays: *The Janitor, Recycle, The Coldest Day of the Year, Malcolm X, The Homecoming* and the musical satire *Black Bart and the Sacred Hills*.

Mr. Wilson received many fellowships and awards, including Rockefeller and Guggenheim fellowships in playwriting, the Whiting Writers Award and the 2003 Heinz Award. He was awarded a 1999 National Humanities Medal by the President of the United States, and received numerous honorary degrees from colleges and universities, as well as the only high school diploma ever issued by the Carnegie Library of Pittsburgh.

He was an alumnus of New Dramatists, a member of the American Academy of Arts and Sciences, a 1995 inductee into the American Academy of Arts and Letters, and on October 16, 2005, Broadway renamed the theater located at 245 West 52nd Street: The August Wilson Theatre. In 2007, he was posthumously inducted into the Theater Hall of Fame.

Mr. Wilson was born and raised in the Hill District of Pittsburgh, and lived in Seattle at the time of his death. He is survived by two daughters, Sakina Ansari and Azula Carmen Wilson, and his wife, costume designer Constanza Romero.

WITHDRAWN